D0868936

The Lord's Prayer

Other books by Romano Guardini
available from Sophia Institute Press

The Art of Praying
Meditations Before Mass
The Rosary of Our Lady
The Living God

Romano Guardini

The Lord's Prayer

SOPHIA INSTITUTE PRESS®

Manchester, New Hampshire

Sophia Institute Press

Box 5284, Manchester, NH 03108

1-800-888-9344

Library of Congress Cataloging-in-Publication Data

Guardini, Romano, 1885-1968.
    [Gebet des Herrn. English]
    The Lord's prayer / Romano Guardini.
      p.   cm.
    ISBN 0-918477-46-8 (alk. paper)
    1. Lord's prayer. I. Title.
BV230.G773   1996
226.9'606 — dc20   96-33548 CIP

97 98 99 10 9 8 7 6 5 4 3 2

Contents

Editor's Note: The biblical references in the following pages are based on the Douay-Rheims edition of the Old and New Testaments. Quotations from the Psalms and some of the historical books of the Bible have been cross-referenced with the differing names and enumeration in the Revised Standard Version, using the following symbol: (RSV =).

Preface

Anyone who undertakes to comment upon the Lord's Prayer joins an illustrious line that goes a long way back. From the first century onward, Christian thinkers and men of prayer have been seeking to explore to its depths this purest expression of Christ's inmost being. They were aware that each of His words is rich in divine treasures; that the purest approach of Christian prayer is manifest in the structure of His thoughts and the movements of His spirit, and that consequently, those who place their trust in these hallowed sentences are participating in that same approach; and that the request "Lord, teach us how to pray,"[1] to which Christ replied with the Lord's Prayer, is thus fulfilled.

We too would wish to explore and comment upon this holy of holies. We feel daunted by the great men who have gone before us; but the words of Revelation call each age to interpret them afresh. That a former age has said great things does not

---

[1] Luke 11:1.

relieve ours of the duty of doing its part. And at a time when we feel so many things shaken to their foundations, we have every reason to grope our way back to the very core of the Christian realities wherein the undisturbed omnipotence of the Redemption reigns.

The Lord's Prayer

"Thy will be done"

The Gateway

Jesus came, as John says, "full of grace and of truth,"[2] filled with all the fullness of the Godhead. He went through the day "doing good."[3] And as He encountered people, as events took shape around Him, He gave His divine response in deeds, doctrine, and instruction — what each moment called for; each the fruit of a specific encounter, original and unique, but nonetheless fraught always with eternal meaning.

In the eleventh chapter of his Gospel, Luke relates: "And it came to pass as Jesus was praying in a certain place, that when He ceased, one of His disciples said to Him: 'Lord, teach us to pray, even as John also taught his disciples.' "[4] We can visualize the situation; we can perceive the faint hint of jealousy of that other teacher and his disciples. But in this human and transitory moment, the Lord speaks those eternal words:

[2] John 1:14.
[3] Acts 10:38.
[4] Luke 11:1.

The Lord's Prayer

"When you pray, say:
'Father' — and Matthew prefixes the 'Our' and adds
'Who art in Heaven' —
'Hallowed be Thy name.'
'Thy kingdom come!'
'Thy will be done on earth as it is in Heaven.'
'Give us this day our daily bread,'
'And forgive us our sins, for we also forgive everyone who is indebted to us' — Matthew has:
'And forgive us our debts, as we also forgive our debtors.'
'And lead us not into temptation' — and Matthew adds:
'But deliver us from evil.' "[5]

And now we look for a gateway into the structure of these sentences, an entrance into their vital core. We find it in the petition, recorded by Matthew, "Thy will be done."

We are exhorted here to ask that God's will be done. So this will must be something that is worth asking for; something precious for which we have to petition with all the earnestness and ardor of prayer; something holy and salutary.

God's will is that which He demands of us and which binds us in conscience. We might perhaps be tempted to think that what is meant here is the "moral law" or our "duty." But we have only to insert these words into a prayer to see that they simply do not fit. The moral law and our duty are no doubt exalted concepts. We must strive to live up to them and to see that others do the same. But who would dream of praying,

---

[5] Luke 11:2-4; Matt. 6:9-13.

"May the moral law be fulfilled" or "May duty be done"? "The will of God" includes the moral law, for it enjoins upon human freedom the highest order, binding upon every conscience. But it is more than that — especially if we take the word in the particular abstract sense it has acquired in the modern age. The will of God is something infinite — a totality. It is something profound, near, living, which concerns us vitally and affects our being to its inmost depths.

God's will is His holy intention for the world and for us. It is His eternal counsel, the fruit of His wisdom, the force of His stern decrees, the loving desire of His heart. Holy in itself, it is the epitome of the divine glory, the divine perfection. And it has the same gravity for us, since whether our existence acquires true purpose and reality or becomes a mere semblance depends upon whether God's will is accomplished in it, or not. If God's will enters into an hour, that hour is valid for eternity; if it does not, that hour is frittered away to no purpose. Such is the will of God as meant in the petition.

Now, if the Christian is to pray that God's will be done, it must be possible that His will may *not* be done. After all, we are not exhorted to pray that the sun may rise. Hence, the petition implies that the fulfillment of the will of God is not something that happens as a matter of course, but, on the contrary, something that is doubtful, perhaps even imperiled.

God's will is that which, according to His decree, should be accomplished in the world. But how is it, in fact, accomplished? That the sun rises and sets, that the stars follow their courses, that substances or forces behave this way or that: all these things are also the will of God. But God's will in these spheres is entrusted to the course of nature. It has the character of inevitability. There is nothing tentative about it. Nothing can happen other than as it happens. But it is quite another matter when it comes to the higher and exalted things. It is altogether different in matters that, according to the grace and will of God, should take their origin in faith and Revelation.

Here, God does *not* wish His will to be actualized with the compelling force of nature. What is to happen here should arise only from man's inner being — from his heart, his intellect, his love, and his free will. No compelling necessity can force what happens. The recognition of the truth, the creation of noble works and of a just order can come about only through the purity of heart and the willing cooperation of man. But this pure and willing spirit is not guaranteed by any compulsion; on the contrary, it is threatened by indolence, vanity, self-seeking, and apathy. Such things as courage, purity, generosity, loyalty to those who trust in us — whatever we call nobility of character — do not arise automatically or by physical laws; nor do the divinely delicate graces of the loving spirit, such as faith, love, humility, and holiness. They must come forth out of the freedom of the heart and the will.

But what a restless, frail, uncertain thing this free will of man is! What strength it has, but also what weakness. How many good, constructive, elevating powers it harbors, but also, alas, how many corrupting, degrading, disruptive forces. Man is prone to evil, and his will goes counter to God's. To the will of God, he answers with a rebellious "I don't want to."

And so God's will is in danger of contradiction. The higher the nature of what He wills, the more His will is imperiled. The nobler the thing that God's will desires, the less assured it is of being done and the more frail, as it were, this divine will appears on earth. Indeed, the holiest effort of God's divine will, the effort coming from His inmost heart, that is, the desire of His redemptive and self-giving love, appears to be singularly ineffective in this world, left to the mercy of every chance; and the probability of its finding fulfillment seems to be very slight. Or am I wrong? When Christ, with all the ardor of His most pure nature, brought the holy will of His Father into the world, what happened? The altogether unthinkable: Christ was taken for a seducer of the people and a criminal, and put to death. Here we see clearly the fate that can befall the will of God in the world, even though every opposition must in the end serve God's designs — just as it was because of man's terrifying disobedience that the Lord died His redeeming death.

And so we can surely understand that the Christian, taught by the spirit of Christ, must feel the threat to the will of God. The Christian knows the ways of the world, and he knows his own ways, and in consequence, he also knows that the will of God may be contradicted.

And there is something else to consider, something that is not easy to express, since it is a mystery that pertains to the essential nature of God's freedom and because our words, which take their meaning and origin from the temporal world, always do it violence. It is this: the will of God, which is directed toward man in the form of destiny, divine decree, encounter, task, and ordeal, can actually be obstructed by man. Man can shut himself up so closely that the will of God cannot approach him. For lack of man's free cooperation,

God's will does not unfold. In consequence, God's intention directed toward a certain person cannot be realized as it would have been if that person had given it scope and possibility. For God does not force man. Providence and destiny do not take the same course with man as the rain and the sun do with the earth; they are linked with man's active willingness. They call forth this willingness and are liberated by and allowed access to it — or they are fettered and hindered by it.

So from this quarter, too, God's will is imperiled.

That it is nevertheless God's almighty and victorious will that shall be vindicated in the end, both in general and in individual matters, is also true; but it is true as a mystery and as a severe trial of man's faith, which, as it were, must enter with the holy will of God into the shadow of weakness, in order to share in its justification on the day of judgment.

So the Christian's concern is engaged for the will of God, which is the highest of the high and the end of all things, and yet, in this temporal world, appears most frail when it wills what is most holy.

∞

Hence the Christian feels responsible for this will and stands up for it. And one might imagine him saying to himself, "If this is the position of the will of God, I will take it upon myself to see that God's will is done!"

But as we think this through, we come to realize that we go counter to the Christian spirit. For the self-will of man cannot substitute for the will of God. God's will is a mystery and can be accomplished by man only through grace. This too becomes clear from the petition, which assumes that God's will is an exalted one well worth our concern. It implies, moreover, that the will of the Almighty is endangered in the world; otherwise it would make no sense to be solicitous about it. But this solicitude turns imploringly to God Himself, which means that the accomplishment of this will must be granted by the same One who demands its fulfillment from us.

Notice how closely the web of mystery is knit.

That concern of the Christian, which is aware of the mysterious nature of the will of God, knows at the same time that this will can be accomplished only by the gracious gift of the same God. The Christian knows that the concern he feels is a reverberation of that first, primal concern that lives in the heart of God Himself; that God does not send His will, which is dear to Him, into the world like a lifeless thing, but, on the contrary, fills it with His power; that God's desire is to love, and that it brings with it the power that makes fulfillment possible. The Christian knows that the appeal of God's will is grace and loving care both for the holy will and for the One appealed to, and that the glory of God and the salvation of mankind are one.

So the Christian knows that in his concern, he is at one with God. And when this concern becomes petition, it has the boundless confidence that it is asking what the heart of God Himself desires.

∞

That the will of God is a command and that we shall one day be judged according to it; that it is at the same time the meaning of all existence; that it is the will of the Almighty and yet is endangered, renounced, and apparently powerless in this world; that it is delivered up to man and yet can be fulfilled by him only through God's grace; that it binds to what should be and is solicitous for the highest good; that it is the responsibility of man and the solemn majesty of God: all of this is interwoven in a profound and holy mystery.

How the Christian mind experiences and accomplishes this is what we choose to call the concern of the Christian.

It is also the gateway we have been looking for, the guide into the Lord's Prayer. It shall open up its abundance to us.

"Our Father Who art in Heaven" (1)

In the foregoing reflections, we looked for a gateway to lead us into the fertile core of the Lord's Prayer, in order that from there, we would be better able to understand the whole. We found this opening in the petition "Thy will be done!" We have seen that God's will, on whose accomplishment the meaning of all existence hinges, is endangered in the world; we have also seen the Christian concern that knows it is responsible for this highest yet frailest good: the mutual understanding into which the Christian, solicitous for the holy will, enters with God Himself. This insight shall disclose to us the riches of the Lord's Prayer. Starting out from it, we shall penetrate the meaning of each separate petition. Not that we have tried to deduce the petitions' content from that first insight; we do not wish to set up any system of instruction. But the petition for the fulfillment of the will of God has revealed to us a disposition of mind, a vital relationship into which God, by His grace, draws man. Proceeding from this, one petition after another shall disclose its meaning to us.

The Lord's Prayer

The prayer begins with the words "Our Father, Who art in Heaven." With these words, it raises its face and its gaze seeks another face, the face of the Father, that eye may meet eye and that the movement of man's heart may find its way to the heart of God.

Of the words of this invocation, we single out the last ones: "Who art in Heaven." We propose not only to think about them, but to live them in spirit. Words are movements — movements of the heart, of the mind. We shall therefore trace the movement that springs up and seeks its paths in the words of the invocation. And we shall allow ourselves to be gripped and led and carried along by it.

First, there is that holy and marvelous "Who." Everyone with religious sensibilities has an awareness of something above and all-pervading. Around us are objects and people, houses and streets, countryside and mountains. Our conscious awareness is filled with these things. Their obtrusive reality engrosses us. But as soon as our inner being is recollected and activated, it perceives — more or less distinctly, more or less strongly — that these are not just things on their own. It perceives that all these things point to something else; that object and person, house and street, countryside and mountains, and all things that live and move are enveloped by something that transcends them. This something is mysterious, yet profoundly familiar: it is holy; it is the Divine. We have the same feeling about human existence, Providence, and destiny. In every human form, in every action and event, there is something that is transcendental, all-pervading, all-embracing; some connection, some point of reference, some meaning: the Divine.

But the words of the Our Father tell us:

You have to deal not merely with "the Divine"; not merely with a mysterious, all-pervading deity, but with a Being; not merely with a something you can feel, but with a Someone you can address; not merely with an authority that touches you, but with a countenance you are called to look upon; not merely with a sense and meaning in things you can feel, but with a heart to which you can turn. For this Divine is the Lord God, and He is such that you can address Him as a person.

∞

Let us not take all of this for granted, however. Let us consider our experience. Is it so easy to focus the indefiniteness of this holy something into the distinctness of the divine countenance? Is it so quickly that we reach awareness of the inner vision that finds Him? Is it only natural that the prayer of our mind, the movement of our heart, reaches up to Him and feels itself to be heard and received, which in itself is felt as an answer? Those who feel this way should indeed be thankful and cherish this gift, for it is a great grace. Most people know how difficult it is for their prayer to gain a foothold, as it were, among the undefined and the incomprehensible.

But quite apart from this experience, the fact that God is someone whom we can address as a person is definitely not something to be taken for granted: it is God's gift. . . .

The Lord's Prayer

God has first called us. He has first addressed me as a person. In doing so He has given me a face of my own, a face whose essential nature it is to turn toward Him. And thus, in addressing God directly, I am capable of seeking in my turn His face.

And now the prayer challenges us to speak to Him as a person, a "who," and to speak to Him directly.

It does not say, "If you want to call upon God, go to such-and-such a place, and there you will find Him," or, "Wait for a certain time, and then you may invoke Him," or, "You must do it in such-and-such a way to succeed in making contact." Nothing of the kind! On the contrary, the Our Father says, in effect, "Simply address yourself to Him who is in Heaven, and your prayer will reach Him. No matter where you are, your words will reach Him. At any hour, your invocation will find Him. Whatever you may experience, whatever may occupy you, your voice can rise, and it will reach God."

We should not take this as a matter of course, however; it most definitely is not. We take it for granted only as long as our thoughts remain earth-bound, as it were. But when we stop to consider it, there is something immeasurably marvelous in the fact that God is accessible from anywhere, at any time, from anything; that the call sent out in the right way never goes astray and always reaches its goal.

∞

Then follow the words "Who art in Heaven." God is everywhere, at every moment and in every situation — but as in Heaven. He is in everything, in all things and in all happenings — but as the One who is in Heaven. God is He who alone is Himself. *Heaven* signifies the way in which the most holy God is with Himself. Heaven is the inaccessibility of God; it is that blessed, inviolable freedom in which He belongs to Himself, as He who is.

We have within us an intimation of Heaven. Something in us senses what the heavenly must be: that it must be infinitely pure and holy; absolutely calm and hidden; strange yet familiar; beautiful and blessed. But this intimation is vague and can be distorted into something aesthetic or sentimental. What is really desired by the "soul destined to be Christian" is fulfilled only by the words of Christ; from the intimacy of the soul; from the depths of one's being and its direction. *Heaven* stands for the otherness of God; yet this otherness constitutes our homeland, with its "eternal mansions."[6]

Hence, the invocation "Who art in Heaven" means that we ourselves are starting from the place where we are, from the hour in which we live, from the things we are engaged in — but that the God we seek is in Heaven, that is, different from all else. We must raise our minds from the earth when we address God, who is in Heaven. We must grant God this otherness. We must admit that He is not like things or like time or like ourselves. We do not prescribe to Him what He is to be like, but are agreed that He is the One who is of Himself. That is the way we want Him. That is the way we seek Him. And we are prepared for the fact that He is different from our expectations, mysterious and unknown. Yet it is precisely in this that He is our homeland, in which "our hearts can rest."[7]

[6] Luke 16:9.

[7] Cf. Matt. 11:29; St. Augustine, *Confessions*, Bk. 1, ch. 1.

∞

And so we dare to address ourselves to God, who is in Heaven, other than our earth. We do not want any God who could be circumscribed by earthly conceptions. We do not want God to be like a human being, like a thing, like the world. We want Him, the living God, who has said, "I am who am."[8] The gravity of Christian thought is intent upon experiencing the true God, and only Him.

But in this we must be on our guard, not only against things and people, but above all against ourselves. Our human nature tries to defend itself against God. The most hidden form of this defense, its most secret weapon, consists in the inclination of our human nature to transform the image of God into the likeness of our own image. And so it makes God innocuous. For then there is no longer the true encounter face-to-face, for man encounters only his own image projected into the clouds. Then it is not with the living God that he speaks, but with himself. The words "in Heaven" say, "I want You, God, as You are in Yourself." And in uttering them, the Christian takes the risk, as it were, of having this God come into his life; of having the everyday tenor of his own life disturbed by the entry of God, the Other, the Inscrutable.

[8] Exod. 3:14.

"Our Father Who art in Heaven" (2)

Rising from anywhere, our call can find God. No matter where it starts from, the movement of the heart can rise and reach God. There is no time schedule; we can go to Him at any hour. There are no conditions stipulated; no events that open the way by their nature or others that close it. Whatever may happen and whatever we may engage in, from anywhere, there is a way that leads to God. This is a great and blissful thought, and to appreciate it fully, one would need to have experienced the utter misery of separation from God.

But all this does not exhaust the substance of the opening invocation of the Lord's Prayer.

∞

From everywhere a way leads to God. Agreed. But can we be quite sure that we are going that way, when we think we are taking it?

There have been innumerable men and women, many of them devout, high-minded, and noble, who were convinced that the Divine resided in many forms, in deities of various kinds. We have only to think of that people to whom our history owes so much — the Greeks. They were devout, more so perhaps than any other people, and more gifted, yet they prayed to many gods — to Zeus, the supreme ruler; to Athena, the goddess of all wise and beautiful things; to the deities of the mysterious and fruitful earth. We must not see this in a frivolous light. To talk of "the poor heathen," as people so often do, can be both priggish and stupid, if the speaker who does so feels smug in his orthodoxy and wonders how on earth other people could believe so much nonsense. In the inmost nature of man — and in the inmost nature of things and indeed of religion itself — there must be something that makes it quite possible for the devout to postulate "gods." Indeed, there is a particular temptation about this, for it opens up certain religious possibilities.

We should do well not to dismiss this thought too scornfully; for what assurance do we have that Europe may not return once more to worshipping other gods? And yet, to be sure, these gods may be quite different from the gods of antiquity.

Other peoples, again, have thought of the Divine in terms of something quite indefinable and intangible — a mysterious Something permeating all things, the mysterious First Cause from which all things arise, the secret meaning underlying all things. And again, these were not inferior or impious people who thought of God in this pantheistic fashion as an impersonal, omniscient being whom they honored with a vague awe and yearning. There is something in the nature of the world, in the essence of things, in the depths of the human soul, that draws man to such a view and makes him respond to this form of piety.

Again, others have conceived of God as a being of such remoteness that the world is nothing to Him; a supreme being who can be worshipped only from an infinite distance, and whom no prayer, no intimacy, no love can reach; with whom there can be no union.

And there are many other forms of misguided religious movements.

Hence, we see that it is quite possible for the religious movement of the heart to get onto a false track. It is quite possible for it to turn to a false image of God. And the possibilities for the falsification of the living reality of God do not arise by chance or from sheer irrationality. On the contrary, they arise from basic things and the essential nature of man himself. They are wrong interpretations of real emotional drives; not haphazard misunderstanding, but violent forces that drive the heart of man, no longer sure of its bearings, in the wrong direction. And these interpretations bring forth not only distortions and subversions, but also great personalities and noble aspirations. Every people has its own particular dangers of going wrong on its way to God and falsifying His image; every age has them; every individual has them, too. They lie in their individual characters, in their particular failings, but also in their strengths.

∽

The Our Father points the way to the "right" God. It says, in effect, "If you want to reach Him, you must seek Him through Him who taught you to pray in these words. You must

19

go to Him, and then with Him, go to God." Paul speaks of "God, who is the Father of our Lord Jesus Christ."[9] If we want to find God, the movement of our heart and mind must mean God as Jesus means Him when He speaks of God. It must turn to Him to whom Jesus turns when He speaks to His Father. It must seek its goal together with Jesus and through Jesus, who has said, "No one comes to the Father except through me."[10]

∞

Therefore, if we ask who God is, the answer is: He with whom Jesus speaks when He speaks to His Father. If we ask what God is like, the answer is: He is as Jesus, in His being and in His actions, revealed Him to be: "He who sees me, sees the Father."[11]

∞

This is not self-evident, and it is not always easy to act accordingly, either.

Someone has complained that Christianity has narrowed the great stream of the heart; has obliged man to make his way to God through the one Christ and forced upon him the special stamp that comes from Christ. The creative originality of religious experience was paralyzed by this, he alleged; the free abundance of its forms was reduced to a homogeneous monotony. This is an argument that calls for an answer. Why should it not be permissible for religious feeling to go its own

---

[9] Cf. Col. 1:3; 1 Pet. 1:3.
[10] John 14:6.
[11] John 14:9.

way, confident that whatever it comes to is good? Why should not the image of God, my conception of God, be permitted to encounter me as my nature and my destiny ordain? Christ answers: Because you can go disastrously astray; because you can arrive at a false image of God. In fact, it can happen that what you believe to be God is only a glorification of yourself or a delusion of the powers of darkness.

At the bottom of these false images of God, of which we have spoken, and underlying the greatness that they may manifest, are darkness and evil, ruin and destruction.

∞

The God toward whom the Lord's Prayer points is called "Father." We have spoken of the Christian concern for the reality of God. This Christian solicitude is also watchful to see that when the Father is spoken of, the right Father is meant.

For there is also a false one. The earlier religions of all the western peoples had a heavenly father — the ruling deity of the all-embracing, illuminating, and activating heavens. By the Greeks, he is called Zeus; by the Romans, Jupiter; by the ancient Germans, Wotan. The forms vary according to the habits of thought of the different peoples among whom they have arisen, but they always designate the same fatherly power, ruling from a throne above. However, what Christ means when He speaks of the Father in Heaven is something quite different.

He does not mean that Something that can be sensed in the universe as an all-embracing, all-pervading, powerful goodness — a feeling that may change in another hour to horror and the impression of cold indifference. Nor is it the radiant power, ruling from above, creating and giving light — the opposite of the dark, brooding, receptive powers of earth that meet and confront it.

What Jesus means is different. It has pleased God, the almighty ruler and author of the world, the Creator and Lord of mankind, to make His creatures His children. It is not by His nature that He is our Father, but by His gracious decree — truly a divine one — made before the beginning of time, that He has become our Father. In the coming of Christ He has called to His creature, "Thou shalt be my son; thou shalt be my daughter."[12] And that is what the devout believer is, not of his own being or of necessity, but through a covenant that has been made. At the same time, this is certainly the fulfillment of the mystery of the will to completion and perfection, which the yearning of God's love has placed in creation from the beginning of time.

Hence, if I approach God as His child and call Him "Father," this is not because of some pantheistic all-pervading sense of the Godhead or some feeling of envelopment, but because I believe in Christ's words.

And I do well to wonder at these words and to ask myself, "How can it be that my Creator and Lord speaks to me and calls me 'my son'?" I will pray to Him: "Teach me to realize that I am Thy son; that I am Thy daughter. Teach me to understand this from Thyself, from what Thou hast done in me, when Thou didst make me Thy child in Baptism."

It does not belong to our nature and our being that we can say "Father" to God; it is by His grace that He has made us so.

---

[12] Cf. Ps. 2:7.

Happy the man who keeps this thought alive in his heart; let him cherish it with gratitude. But many do not have this living certainty — or not yet. And so it is our care as Christians that the mystery of the fatherhood of God should remain pure and not become confused with something else. It is therefore better that we should go on wondering and marveling over the incomprehensible, better that we should go on striving with difficulty to learn from the heart of Jesus how to speak to God as Father, rather than that this most profound and holy article of our Faith should drift into vagueness or become falsified.

It would indeed be easier to let the heart follow its inclination; to think vaguely of the heavenly Father as of the far-flung heaven spanning a summer landscape, or to conjure up from somewhere the feeling of being safe and cherished. But the Lord's Prayer warns us: Beware! It is not by integration with the natural world that you are God's child, but by grace and faith.

Faith, however, is not only a blessed certainty; it is also a matter of practice and self-conquest. You must therefore learn to speak to God as Father. You must learn it from the attitude of Christ; you must learn it from the way in which He Himself says "Father"; in which He leads us by His parables and sermons to say "Father" to God. You must conform the attitude of your heart to this teaching, and then let it guide the movements of your inmost soul.

∞

From the tuition that the heart receives in such practice, the Christian attitude of the child to the Father — or, to be more correct, of the son or daughter to the Father — gradually grows. Through such schooling, we should grow to be sons and daughters of God. We should grow to the full maturity of adult existence; to the strength and stature of those whom God has called to enter into an understanding with Him; into that agreement in which the Christian's concern for God's holy will is united to His omnipotence.

This engenders an attitude of great gravity. This arises, not from nature, but from the sincerity and strength of the individual; not from vague, poetic feelings, but from the explicitness and responsibility of faith. And what began as watchfulness and effort, perhaps as narrowness and compulsion, too, gradually becomes a new freedom: the freedom of mind and heart that comes from contact with the living God, the Father of our Lord Jesus Christ.

∞

But there is yet another word in the opening invocation — namely, *our*. We are directed, then, to take others with us when we come to the Father in the Lord's Prayer.

Once more something in us resists. Does one always have to be with other people? Must I always be in a crowd? After all, I'm myself; I exist in my own right! What of the world if I am not myself? Surely it is in the essential nature of the person to be a separate being? How do other people concern me when I come to God, since doing so, after all, really means coming to myself? Are not the words "God and my soul, and the world well lost" an ever valid statement?

The Our Father replies with a warning. It reminds us that consciousness of oneself and one's uniqueness can be pagan. The "sovereign individual" does not exist. The only really sovereign person is God. Man, by contrast, exists only as a social being, together with all his fellows, integrated with them in the interplay of word and action, the unity of guilt and destiny. The Our Father makes clear to us that the exaggerated individual consciousness of modern times is a depredation; for the growing emphasis on "the person" and the "human person" has tended to take over, first imperceptibly and later with increasing clarity, the image and dimension of the divine Person.

As we say not "my Father" but "our Father," we are to repudiate all this and testify to the incontrovertible community of created men. Indissolubly and of my nature I am a man among men; but by grace, I am a Christian "among many brethren,"[13] bound to all the others in the community of guilt and redemption; in the unity of the Mystical Body of Christ; in the expectation of that eternal life that shall be lived by "a great multitude which no man could number."[14]

Therefore, when I pray, it has to be done in such a manner that I include my fellow beings, either explicitly or in the form of my approach.

∞

But was the above-mentioned objection altogether wrong? Something in it was justified. It arose from concern for the uniqueness of the Christian person.

God has not addressed Himself to man in a group. He does not sweepingly call an assembled crowd His children. God

[13]Rom. 8:29.
[14]Rev. 7:9.

does not look upon us *en masse*. He addresses Himself to each individual, to every single person. And He is there absolutely for each one. God is there absolutely and completely for me; to me He turns with all that He is. He knows no compartments. He turns toward me completely, and not according to a blueprint applicable for all, but in special concern for me, who, even while earnestly renouncing all pride, cannot give up my claim to uniqueness. His person in His uniqueness turns to my most individual self — even though this human individual self is completely and in all things a gift from God.

Therefore, when I approach Him, I come as my unique self, in the knowledge that there is no duplicate of me; and my words, which I speak to God, are not spoken by anyone else, because what He gives to me is given only to me. An exclusiveness exists between Him and me, and a secret into which no one else can enter. The words "God and my soul, and the world well lost," spoken in Christendom from the earliest times up to the present, are still valid. They have their verification in that prophecy of Revelation that says that "to him who overcomes," a white pebble shall be given, "and upon the pebble a new name written, which no one knows except him who receives it."[15]

That is true, and it is just as true as communion is true. The same humility that relinquishes the arrogant claim to the natural right as a person is at the same time the ground of the awareness of a person's unique relationship with God alone. But in the process the communion itself becomes changed. The communion I take with me to God in the Our Father is

[15]Rev. 2:17.

no longer that of a group. In prayer, I am not just part and parcel of an indiscriminate multitude.

True, there are many, countless many, the "very great multitude" of the children of God "which no man could number," down through all the ages and nations — "all the brethren"[16] — but each of them stands in the mystery of his uniqueness and individual relationship to the Father. Each of them exists only once. And so the Christian plural stands for something quite different from mere multiplicity, just as it is also quite different from the concept of species, of sharing the same nature. In the Christian "we" there is union and differentiation, fellowship and individual dignity, close association and the privacy of reserve.

[16] Acts 15:3.

"Hallowed be Thy name"

In our first consideration, we looked for a way into the fabric of thought and the spiritual attitude of the Lord's Prayer, and we found it in the petition that God's will be done; in the Christian's concern with what is God's, and in his collaboration with God in this solicitude. Further, it was made clear to whom the movement of the prayer was directed — namely, to the divine Person in Heaven. And we saw that the way leads through Christ, that He whom Christ calls Father is He to whom our prayer is to be directed.

Now we begin with the first petition — namely, "Hallowed be Thy name."

∞

This petition concerns the name of God, that is to say, a word. But when we reflect more carefully on what a word signifies, we plumb to great depths.

A word is something formed by sound, the vibration of the air, the movement of the lips and throat. But this describes only its most external aspect. "Word" is a many-layered thing. It is a body that also has a mind, a soul. Its "mind" is the meaning carried by the sound-form, the association of ideas that people have thought and expressed in the word. Its "soul" is the response it strikes in the heart. In this union of the physical and mental, every word contains a general meaning of universal application, something special that is more closely restricted, and finally the ultimate refinement of meaning that makes it the property of one individual only.

What a fleeting thing a word is — at one moment, not yet there, then spoken and come into being, to fade away immediately and disappear. Yet on closer scrutiny, we realize that is not so. The words *tree* and *book* and *friendship* were in existence before I spoke them. I did not create them; they were already there before I was born. I learned them from my parents and teachers. Words and their combination, namely, speech, are not only things the individual utters as the expression of his inmost being; they are also living symbols, forms full of meaning, in which being becomes audible; forms into which our existence is called so that it becomes intelligible and is in turn molded by them. We form words, and they form us. We are our language; it is as if it had a separate existence, confronting us and making us what we are. Language forms a world, an order of existence into which the individual is born and in which he lives. It envelops him, permeates him, forms him. Words reach down into our inmost being. We not only speak in words, but also think in them. If we examine the matter closely, we notice that our thoughts are clothed in words from their very first inception. Actually, we can think only in terms of speech, not otherwise. From the very roots of our being, we live in words and are made what we are by them. Words are the rails on which our lives run, the shapes of our existence. Words, fleeting forms though they be, are strong. They assert themselves with incredible force. Peoples may have died out long ago, but their language may still live. A city may be destroyed, its builders forgotten; there may no longer be a trace of life in it, but names may have survived.

Words are power. Words have come like a tornado, torn people away from their accustomed ways, and led them up to the heights. Words have fallen like flames of fire into souls and called them forth to great deeds, releasing creative depths and causing great works to proceed from them. Words have made men free, given strength, awakened confidence, given joy. Words have wounded; have bitten in and remained stuck like barbed hooks; have poisoned and destroyed.

Now, all the languages of mankind have a word that means the Supreme Being from whom all things come; to whom all things refer back; who gives a meaning to all things; to whom all things tend — the word *God*. It has been said — and it is a deep thought — that this word was not invented by historical man, but that, together with the idea it expresses, it came with man from Paradise and is now part of his speech, among the other words, to remind, move, teach, and guide him.

But something very special has happened with this word. At a certain point in the history of mankind, God called upon man and revealed Himself to him, when He spoke to Abraham, to the patriarchs, to Moses. He revealed Himself to man as the Lord of history, who comes in His divine freedom and calls upon man. And He made His covenant with man. At that time He took possession of the word *God* and made it His name; and not just as we understand it when we speak of other "names." By *names*, we mean words that pertain to this or that thing or person; this country or this person as distinguished from others. But that is not the original meaning of *name*. *Name* in the original sense means more than a mere designation: it embodies the essential nature of the person named. The name is something mysterious; it stands for the bearer himself.

Now, this mysterious thing, which remains suspended in vagueness in the case of people and things, God has sealed and destined for Himself. He has Himself entered into His name, as it were. From now on, He Himself dwells in His name. When He said of the temple, "My name shall be there,"[17] that meant: "I myself shall be there." And when it was said, "Thy name has been called over me,"[18] that meant, in effect: "Thou hast called; Thou hast turned to me; Thou art coming to me." God's name came, then, and joined the other words and became a part of the language. And there stands the name of God, and with it God Himself, in the midst of human history. It became part of that image-world, namely, language, which takes hold of people and places its imprint on them; it entered into man and worked in him, right down to the roots of his being.

But God's commandment ordered that His name should not be taken in vain. Reverence for the holy name of God lived in the Jewish people and placed its seal on them. This name in which God dwelt, as it were, in the language of man,

[17] 2 Paralip. 7:16 (RSV = 2 Chron. 7:16).
[18] Jer. 15:16.

was invested with such awe by the Jews that for fear of dese-
crating it, they no longer dared to speak it, but replaced it by
another name, "the Lord."

∞

So it is that the name of God, in which He has taken up
His dwelling, is in the world.

In this, His name, God moves through the language of
man, through his heart and mouth and destiny; and the holy
name shares the fate of all words. It is transient, at the mercy
of the fluctuations of existence. It is mighty; it works and
forms; it is held in honor, and it is misused; it is made an object
of reverence and adoration, but also an implement of cursing.
It is spoken in prayer and benediction, but it is also spoken
thoughtlessly, blasphemously, doubtfully, destructively. Yes, indeed! It has even come to this, that the holy name circulates
among men like a shadow. "My God, yes!" someone says; or,
"Oh, my God!" But if you were to ask him, "Do you believe in
God, then?" he would answer, "Well, no, not really, but one
just says that." And so the name of God drifts without meaning through the speech of man, like a ghost, or rather, like an
exile, like an unknown person in a strange land.

And now we are admonished in the Our Father: You must
realize that you have a duty in regard to the name of God.

It does not merely say: You should hold it in honor. It says,
in effect: You must take care of it. You must realize how holy,
how powerful, how homeless, and how abandoned it is. You
must look after it, and you must do so, moreover, in a manner
that is possible only to those who have faith: namely, in
conjunction and agreement with God Himself, begging Him

to grant that the holiness of His name may be felt; that it may find a place in the hearts of men; that it may be held holy among them.

∽

But how is this to be done?

It is done by using it not blasphemously but with reverence; not in doubt but in faith; not in cursing but in blessing; not destructively but constructively; not lightly but seriously; not in evil thoughts but in good ones.

Yet that is not all. The final injunction, however, we cannot express otherwise than by repeating that the name of God should be "hallowed." For the sacred is the conclusive. One cannot explore beyond it. One can only feel it, consent to it, imbibe it — or resist it. The name of God is holy: it stands for the special quality of His living being; all that is proper to Him alone; the mysterious, the unknowable, the inaccessible; the familiarity of our final home, and all that we could possibly say to express the absolute, the ineffable, the immeasurable, which is His very Self. This is what we are to hallow. We are to acquire a disposition and an attitude attuned to the holy, responding to it because it comes from the holy. With this deep, tender, inward, strong sense of the sacred, we are inwardly to embrace the name of God. In our hearts, we are to kneel before this holy name, and clasp our hands around it, and watch over it, and so do our part to see that it is not abandoned and rejected.

This is a wholly divine solicitude, and it can make us holy. The name could become a power within us; it could permeate us and transform us. And so in the Our Father, we pray: Let this mystery be revealed to me. Awaken in me a solicitude for my daily bread, for my loved ones, for my work, for all that is worthy and important. But above all, do Thou awaken in me a solicitude for Thee and Thine; for Thy holy name and its glory; and in this solicitude, make me one heart and one soul with Thee.

∞

How clearly it is indicated here what being a Christian implies! The second of the Ten Commandments binds us not to take the name of God in vain. That was a law, and the people who received that law were formed by God by means of it. Then Christ came, and the new life that had come through Him is made clear in that petition of the Our Father about which we have just been thinking. Here again the matter in question is the holiness of the name of God, as in the Law; but what God desires of us He does not pronounce as a law, but entrusts to man as solicitude for something high and holy, and man is thereby called to cooperation with God Himself.

The Second Petition

"Thy kingdom come"

The second petition of the Lord's Prayer leads us into the very core of what lay nearest to the heart of Jesus. In the form in which it is most used, the words are "Thy kingdom come!" But this is not an absolutely exact translation of the words. Actually it should be "May Thy kingdom arrive" or "May Thy kingdom come." If we say them this way, we feel their vital sense distinctly. There is expectation in them, as well as yearning. Something salutary is far away, and the petition implores that it may come. There is a movement in process, and the longing urges that it may be accomplished. This distant, longed-for, and pleaded-for something, the kingdom of God — what is it?

∞

If we want to realize what its first, unique awakening was like, we must read the Gospels, especially those of Matthew, Mark, and Luke. The first words that are reported of Jesus, as soon as He began His ministry, are "The kingdom of God is at hand! Repent and believe in the gospel."[19] What gospel? Why, of course, the one that announces the nearness of the kingdom of God. These are the joyful tidings — that God's kingdom, which was far away, is now at hand. But people are admonished with joyous urgency: Discern the hour. See what is coming. Open your hearts to it. And implicit in the words is an anxiety lest the time be missed.

Again and again Jesus speaks of the kingdom of God in His parables. If we take them as they were told, in all their fresh originality, if we try to understand what they mean, we soon notice that the "kingdom of God" cannot be reduced to a single concept. It is something mighty, pervasive, penetrating, operative, multiform. Its plenitude has to be grasped by contemplation and thought. Our thought must be able to endure its complexity and grasp its manifold richness as a whole. But we must never try to force it into fixed conceptions, for as soon as we try to do so, its real character disappears, and the whole concept becomes enfeebled.

In one of the parables, the kingdom of God is compared to a treasure hidden in a field. A man — probably a tenant farmer — is plowing the field, and suddenly his plowshare hits something hard. He finds a crock full of coins and jewelry, perhaps hidden from some enemy long ago. He quickly covers it up again and turns all his efforts to acquiring that field. Forthwith he sells all his tools and belongings because he knows that by doing so, he will acquire something more precious than all he gives for it.[20] Similarly, the parable of the

---

[19] Mark 1:15.
[20] Matt. 13:44.

pearl: a merchant sees it somewhere, recognizes its value, and sells all he has to acquire it, for his gain is very much greater than what he stakes.[21] Here the kingdom of Heaven represents something infinitely precious. Man is urged to stake all upon gaining it, and is assured that whatever he may give will be a small thing compared with his gain. In fact, it is particularly emphasized that it is a question of giving all. But this all — it is much because it is "all" on the part of the giver — is a small thing compared with the infinite value of the kingdom that is acquired.

Again, the kingdom of Heaven is a mustard seed, the smallest of all seeds. It is put in the earth, it germinates, and from it grows a shrub so big that the birds come and nest in it.[22] Here the kingdom of God is represented as something smaller than anything else, something almost invisible, insignificant to the point of nothingness in the midst of the big, brutal realities of the world. But it has in it a mighty capacity for expansion, and when it is given scope, it grows into something capacious and widely embracing, which can afford a home and a safe shelter.

Again, the kingdom of Heaven is a fishing net. It is cast out and then drawn in to land; and the fishermen sit down and sort out the catch. The "bad" fish — the ones it is impermissible to eat — they throw away; the others they carry home.[23] Here the kingdom of God is something that comes to many, that touches and embraces great numbers. But many of these

[21] Matt. 13:45-46.
[22] Matt. 13:31-32.
[23] Matt. 13:47-48.

do not fit in with it; they do not prove good and are ejected again. Others belong in it and are kept.

Similarly, the parable of the weeds in the tillage. The kingdom of God is in the world; it is interwoven with human history. It embraces people of different kinds; events follow one after another; connections and interplays, influences and dependencies, all mesh one with the other. And so no one can distinguish those who really belong to the kingdom of God from those who do not, any more than one can separate from the wheat in the tillage field the weeds whose roots and stalks are inextricably entangled with the good growth. The time of growth and ripening must be over, the field must be mown and the harvest brought home, history must end, the Last Judgment must come. Only then will the separation take place.[24]

Then again, the kingdom of God is a leaven that a woman takes and buries in a measure of flour. The leaven works its way through the dough so that the bread is soft and light and rises properly.[25] Here the kingdom of God is something that operates inwardly, working its way through from one particle to the next, affecting and transforming the whole.

∞

The Lord spoke other parables, too, and one image follows another. To express in a few words what the kingdom of God really is, is simply impossible. Perhaps we may express it in this way. The kingdom of God means that God rules, directly and powerfully; that God, in the freedom of His love, has forgiven

[24] Matt. 13:24-30.
[25] Matt. 13:33.

sin, and that man, sanctified by the holiness of Christ, belongs entirely to God. The kingdom of God means that His truth illumines the mind, and there is now no longer a weary search, or a wretched, paltry patchwork, but an openly shining, holy plenitude; that the powerful meaning of the holy truth sustains man, and that he is really and inwardly at one with this truth, which liberates, satisfies, and beautifies; which exceeds all sensible things, yet keeps and guards every heart; which rules in inaccessible glory, yet is his tender friend; with which he is really and inwardly one. The kingdom of God means that God is felt in His holiness, perceived in His majesty; that man has surrendered his freedom to Him and that God now reigns, with his joyful consent, in his will and in all his powers. It means that the intimacy and preciousness of the things of God are experienced; that the ineffable bliss of His beauty and sweetness is tasted in the heart and felt to the depths of one's being. The kingdom of God means that He, the Father, the Brother, the Friend, is near, in the depths of the spirit, in the core of the heart; that love rules perceptibly in our goings and our comings, our dispensing and our receiving; that the whole of existence is transfigured by it; that while everything is transmuted into this one thing, the essential beauty and character of each blossoms forth. The kingdom of God means that God becomes distinct to us in His reality and fullness; that He rules in all things, and that the creature is in Him, one with Him, and for this very reason, is free to be himself.

When the Lord came, this kingdom was near. God had "come" so near that He was ready to burst forth everywhere, to draw all things to Himself and to the freedom of the community of God. People were urged to "do penance,"[26] to turn away from their degradation and perversity and toward Him who called to them. And one can imagine that if this had been done, something would have happened. We recall the prophecies of Isaiah and reflect that at that time, when "the time was fulfilled,"[27] the kingdom might really have begun. But people did not believe. They let the time pass by. The hour of darkness came, and the kingdom seemed to be in retreat.

However that may be, by the petition in the Our Father the Lord indicates that the kingdom of God is not "here," as something finished and arrested. It is coming. It is in a continuous state of coming, and we are to pray that it may arrive.

The kingdom of God is something that is directed toward us, as it were; that presses forward toward us — to each of us individually and to each in his communion with all.

It presses forward, but in no way does it force its arrival. It cannot arrive, in any case, for it can come only in freedom. Man must open himself to it. He must believe. He must prepare himself. He must strain toward it with eager longing. He must be courageous with the kingdom of God and let it in; he must surrender himself to it. But if he shuts himself up, if he remains indifferent or resists, or rebels and refuses obedience, then the kingdom slips away from him. The power of Almighty God works in it, and it works only in freedom and only if freedom opens itself to it. If this does not happen, then the power of God is powerless, as it were. If man becomes immersed in the

26 Matt. 4:17.
27 Cf. Mark 1:15.

happenings of the day; if he becomes entangled in his passions; if he loses his heart to his fellow beings and his possessions, then the kingdom, finding no place in him, recedes and vanishes.

Once more we are faced with the mystery we have met before: God is the Lord; His wisdom penetrates all things; His will is all-powerful, and yet He comes with all the certainty of His love and wishes to realize His kingdom. He yearns for His creatures, and "His delights are to be with the children of men."[28] He desires to accomplish that mystery of His love, the union of humanity in Him, and He desires it with divine earnestness — but faced with man's free will, He seems mysteriously weak.

∞

And so the Our Father admonishes us once more to concern ourselves with this great thing upon which everything depends for ourselves and for the whole world, and which nevertheless seems to be so much in doubt in this same world. But our concern is not to express itself in that personal activism that would seek by its own efforts to get justice done, but rather in collaboration with Him who alone can grant that the threatened kingdom may be realized — namely, with God. We are to pray to Him that His kingdom may come.

∞

Now, what is it like when the kingdom of God really reaches a human being? The saints reveal this to us, especially

[28]Prov. 8:31.

The Lord's Prayer

St. Francis of Assisi. Much that is great can be told of him, but above all else, it can be said that he became in a special manner the interpreter of the gospel. In a peculiarly clear and forceful way, everything about him tells us what it is like when Christ's words are fulfilled in a person.

The kingdom of God surrounds Francis with an openness, a holy nearness, a rich, active fullness. He is utterly human; he is human in a particularly beautiful and profound sense in that God works in him unhindered. But around him the world is different from what it is around others. Legends are told of him, but is it really so important whether the birds came to him or not; or whether the fish listened to him; or whether the wolf of Gubbio laid its paw in his hand? That such things could be told of him, though, is proof that around him everything was different from its ordinary self. For the kingdom of God had been able to reach him.

It did not reach him once and for all, but did so anew again and again. With him, the kingdom of God was not something finished and arrested. With him, too, it was in a state of continuous coming; and if Francis had regarded himself as perfect and had settled down to a state of fixed possession, he would have lost the most precious thing he had. The mysterious fullness that Christ calls the kingdom of God streamed into him continually. And continually he opened himself to it and received it anew.

The Third Petition

"Thy will be done on earth as it is in Heaven"

In the interpretation of the Our Father we are back once more to that third petition, "Thy will be done on earth as it is in Heaven," in which we sought and found the key to the spirit and basic approach of the whole prayer. Let us pause at it once more, but not to meditate upon what the will of God is: that mightiest of powers, which has created all things and yet seems so weak in the world it has created; that highest thing in which lies the meaning of all things and that nevertheless is continually in danger of being lost, for which reason the Christian is urged to make it his care and enters into an understanding with God Himself, begging Him to grant the fulfillment of His holy will.

Instead, we shall try to understand what the petition means when it asks that God's will be done "on earth as it is in Heaven."

This petition is stretched between Heaven and earth, as it were; between the divine above and the human below. But what does *Heaven* mean? And what does *earth* mean? What have they got to do with each other?

If we ask an educated person today what Heaven is, he might reply, "The heavens are the space in which the celestial bodies move." The answer is correct; it is the answer of natural science; but it is of no use to us here. We cannot insert that Heaven into the petition of the Our Father, because out there, in cosmic space, the will of God is not fulfilled any better by the constellations than it is on earth by its substances and natural forces. If we ask a child, "Heaven — what is that?" he will probably point upward, saying, "That up there!" Again, this is a correct answer, the answer of visible appearance. But neither can it help us with the Our Father, for in this case there is no "above" and "below" to which we can point with our finger.

But it may also be that the answer, whether given by a child or by some devout believer, may prove to be different and run somewhat this way: Heaven is the place where God lives; or, Heaven is the place from which the Redeemer came; or, Heaven is the eternal dwelling God has prepared for us. These answers would have come from a different source — neither from natural science, nor from fairy tales, nor from the evidence of the eyes, but from faith. They would point in the right direction. If we want to know what Heaven is, we must ask Revelation. We must ask Him who came down to us on earth from Heaven, and returned to Heaven again — namely, Jesus Christ.

Now, He speaks of Heaven not as of something set apart, but as of something bound up with the living existence of God. When Jesus speaks of the Father, He almost always adds "in

Heaven" to the words "our Father." And again, Christ connects Heaven with man as his blessed goal and final condition. Thus, we are urged to "lay up treasures in Heaven,"[29] which means we are to place in Heaven the goal and standard of our thoughts and actions, the fruits and form of the final perfection our lives are to show. Paul follows up this thought of Christ when he reminds us that "our citizenship is in Heaven,"[30] where Christ has returned and sits at the Father's right hand.

We shall therefore be correct in saying that Heaven is the dwelling place of God. It is that place where God is with Himself; not a place existing in itself "in" which God is, but the "inaccessible light in which God dwells";[31] the radiant inaccessibility, so brilliant that it blinds the human eye, in which God dwells with Himself. Heaven signifies God insofar as He dwells with Himself, freely and completely reserved to Himself and Himself alone.

∞

Now, when it is said that the will of God is done in this Heaven, by whom is it done there? By God Himself.

The Holy Spirit is in essence the fulfillment of the will of God. In the Holy Spirit, God fulfills His will of ceaseless self-giving, in that the Father gives Himself to the Son and the Son gives Himself back to the Father, and is with Him, "in Him,"[32] as John says, divinely self-surrendered, yet eternally

[29] Matt. 6:20.
[30] Phil. 3:20.
[31] 1 Tim. 6:16.
[32] Cf. John 10:38.

preserved and sheltered. The impenetrable mystery of the blessed unity of self-giving and self-keeping, this accomplishment of the divine will in the Holy Spirit — this is the very root and essence of Heaven, its inmost sanctuary and the calmest sea of its peace.

It is from here that it is granted that the will of God be done by the creature. For God's will — which is the will to give Himself in love — has created the world in order that He, divinely given, might be in it; and in order that the world, in giving itself back to Him as a free gift, should reach up to Him and become one with Him in love. The created beings in whom this will finds perfect fulfillment, namely, the angels and the blessed, are thereby in the union of love with God and admitted to Heaven. They are with Him there, by the grace of the Holy Spirit, sharing in the divine presence in which the Son, giving Himself back to Himself, is reunited with the Father. The will of God is fulfilled in them now by what they are; for they are living by the Spirit of God, in the eternal perfection of their essential being. And they go on fulfilling it in all their works and actions, without effort or compulsion, from the deepest, most essential need of their natures, purely because in their blessed state they cannot do otherwise. This fulfillment of the divine will takes the form of divine ease, beauty, and joy. It is the eternal "canticle of praise."[33]

In Heaven, the divine will is done fully and completely. And how could it be otherwise, since those blessed beings are possessed in spirit by the glory of God? If we do not fulfill the will of God, it is because we do not recognize His holy truth,

[33] Ps. 39:4 (RSV = Ps. 40:3).

or because His will seems unimportant to us, or because we misunderstand it. But the blessed in Heaven are penetrated by the Holy Spirit Himself with the divine fullness, and so they can do nothing other than, as Paul says, *aletheuein en agape* — the words are almost untranslatable — "do the truth," or "be the truth," "the truths in love."[34] We fail to do the holy will because the reality of the world seems to us stronger and more attractive, because we feel some worldly value more closely and more alluringly. The hearts of the blessed, on the contrary, are flooded with the divine perfection, and no power on earth can wrest them away from its power and sweetness. And so they cannot do other than fulfill the eternal will of God, and in that consists their blessedness. They have reached the holy state of being unable to sin; and so the divine will is fulfilled in Heaven in absolute perfection. It is the air they breathe. It is the blood that pulses through them. It is the visible content and force of their existence. And so they cannot do other than love it, and their love is their freedom.

And now the petition speaks of the earth. But again, what is the *earth*? This planet upon which we live and the things on it — but seen in relation to man and from the standpoint of his existence; in relation to man, moreover, as he is now, in the time of his sinfulness and his pilgrimage. This creature knows but little of God. His heart is not inundated with the power of the divine love. Therefore he can forget God, overlook Him, lose sight of Him with his mind and intellect.

[34]Eph. 4:15.

The Lord's Prayer

∞

There is a mystery about creation. God made the world, and He did it with divine gravity. What He created, man and things, are not appearances. God did His work well and truly. In creating, He did not sketch; He made the nonexistent existent. He created everything in the round, as it were, to stand and to last. Then He gave each thing its freedom to live in accordance with its true being. But what, in the case of things, amounted to being left free within the framework of their own reality and essential nature, in man means being left free to use his free will. He is left free to stand on his own. (This is an oversimplification; we shall amplify it later on; but first listen to this: let it sink in; only then will what follows be fully appreciated.)

All this constitutes the gravity of creation and involves the possibility of a terrifying decision, for man is confronted by the thought: "This thing, which is so real and so substantial, and I, who live and act on my own responsibility — we together are all-sufficing. We can dare to think that only we exist!" The very mastery with which God has created the world gives occasion to the danger that the world will misunderstand itself and think it can do without God. That would be sin. And this sin has happened, and is happening all the time.

∞

Now we feel renewed within us the anxiety of the Christian, his fear for his own salvation and that of the world. Man is prone to misinterpret creation's masterly perfection and to abuse it by sin. This would be to ruin it. For the reality that has now been released, that independence of operation — and now comes the supplementary remark referred to above — that essential nature and existence only exist, when all is said and done, in God. Not near Him, not without Him, but "in God we live, and move, and have our being."[35] How this is, no one can understand; but man's being in the world really and truly is only from God and in God. What is more, it subsists in a state of movement toward Him. Man exists not as a perfect and completed being, but in a state of movement toward God. He becomes more and more real and complete, the nearer he comes to God. This is the movement by which the creature gives himself back to Him who, in creating him, first gave Himself to man. But it is just this movement of the creature toward the Creator that is nothing other than the fulfillment of the will of God. To do God's will means to come nearer to Him. Only in doing so does the creature become, in the ultimate sense, real. And by doing so, the creature is meant to reach his place with God, and have part by grace in His holy self-indwelling in Heaven.

That God has given to His creation its essential character of freedom and continued independent existence signifies in itself, at the same time, the call "Come to me!"

What does a mother yearn for, and what is her supreme delight? She has given life to her child; she has given him out of herself the capacity to live and breathe as an independent being. Now the child is growing up; the little human life is unfolding of itself, becoming the focal point from which the great reality surrounding him is only beginning to appear as

[35] Acts 17:28.

the real "world." What is the mother's supreme delight now? That this child turns back to her with his first smile, his first word, his first step; that the union now coming anew into being by love between this little child and his mother is so much deeper and greater than that first union out of which it has come! In the same way, God yearns for His creation, for humanity, to turn back to Him by word and look, by the movement of its love, to the union of Heaven; in other words, He yearns that His will be done. And the Christian makes it his care that this will really is done.

Let us suppose, now, that the child did not smile back at his mother, but shut himself off from her; did not speak to her or try to toddle back to her, but remained silent, turned the other way, and went off on his own. We feel at once what cold, unnatural behavior that would be, and how it must chill the mother's heart. But it is beyond all comparison more terrible when creation turns away from God by sin. Then — we speak in the words of Genesis, where it says that God was "touched inwardly with sorrow of heart"[36] when men went their wicked ways, and He sent the deluge — this is a divine grief, the sorrow of the unrequited love of God; sorrow for the fate of His creation, which He loves and which is going into darkness, into death, into nothingness.

∞

Hence, Christ, who "came to save that which was lost,"[37] teaches us to pray as follows: "Thy will be done on earth as it

---

[36] Gen. 6:6.
[37] Luke 19:10.

is in Heaven"; that God may grant that, as His will is done where men have returned home to union with Him and are inundated with His light and love, so, too, may it be done here below, where everything still hangs on the terrible decision as to whether creation is rightly understood, whether that divine masterpiece is interpreted as a call and an impulse to return home to God or as a reason for forsaking Him.

The prayer asks that His will be done here on earth, where we do not see His light, just as if we did see it — namely, by faith. It asks that although we have not seen, we may love.

"Give us this day our daily bread"

We now turn to the second part of the Lord's Prayer; to those simple petitions in which the realities and needs of our daily existence find expression.

But let us not take this simplicity too simply. What is expressed in it is everyday life, but it is the daily life of the Christian: in other words, the life of the person who lives by what was brought into the world by Christ. Hence the petitions of the second part derive their meaning from those of the first. If we take them by themselves, they drift into irrelevance, but if we understand them from the premise of the first sentences of the prayer, their very simplicity opens up into a bottomless depth.

This is the case right at the start, with the first of them: "Give us this day our daily bread."

We encounter this petition very often in our ordinary, all too ordinary life, from the lips of the half-believing, the indifferent, and the unbelieving. So we have every reason to ask whether these words, spoken so lightly and so often, are really meant as the Lord meant them. For the meaning He put into them was definitely not self-evident, but quite the opposite — it had something of mystery and hazard, which made the petition an expression of that faith that literally "overcomes the world"[38] by making a place in it for the new world that will come from God.

∞

In the petition, there is one word that in itself is enough to startle us. It is not, as a rule, translated very exactly. In the Greek there is a word about which scholars are not clear, because it occurs only once: *epiousios* is what the bread is called for which the petition asks. The most exact translation would seem to be "that for the coming day." If we take as our basis the text of Matthew, this is the petition: "Give us this day our daily [supersubstantial] bread."[39]

Accordingly, it is not for the "daily" bread in the ordinary sense that we pray. It is not as if "its bread" were assured to every day, and now the petition came and asked for what belonged to this particular day. On the contrary, here someone asks for the bread for tomorrow. He is living today, taking the step for the present day, and asking for his food for the next day. The next day is not yet urgent today. Tomorrow it will be urgent, when the step between has been traversed. Then, when the new hour strikes, the petition will rise to the lips again. So we feel that there is a hint in this petition that nothing is assured. Life is to be taken trustfully, hour by hour, as it comes.

[38] Cf. 1 John 5:4.
[39] Matt. 6:11.

At any rate, however the petition may be worded, it refers us to what underlies the Christian day and the Christian trust: the mystery of Divine Providence.

∞

But what does *Providence* mean?

The Christian life has expressed itself in certain words of the language. But the Christian language — the language in which are enshrined the mystery, the hidden forces, the joys, and the desires of that life — has come into some rough usage in the course of time, particularly in the last two centuries. The Christian existence has drifted into worldliness and has changed its words along with itself. Nowadays, words that originated in the holy sphere of Christian faith and love circulate everywhere in the current coin of conversation, but they bear little trace of their origin — sometimes a remnant, a vibration, or a mere breath; otherwise they have become worldly. This has also happened to the holy word *Providence*.

In itself, it means the inmost mystery of Christ. But a temporal quality has been given to it. If we consider carefully what is really meant in current usage by the word *Providence*, we shall find that it is applied to a concept we may roughly call "world order": in other words, something that orders everything and arranges everything nicely and sensibly, so that all things, and consequently mankind with them, are coordinated in a rational way, that is to say, in accordance with nature. To this way of thinking, if wise "nature" is allowed its way and if man behaves rationally and in accordance with the laws of nature, all will be well. In the eighteenth and nineteenth centuries, a whole philosophy — in fact, a whole doctrine of economics and social welfare — evolved on the basis of this way of thinking.

But this allegedly rational universal order, which claims to guarantee the welfare of man, is a very vulnerable affair. We have indeed experienced what it has produced: the World War and the chaos that followed it. However, quite apart from the fact that it does not correspond at all with this "order," what Jesus means by *Providence* is something absolutely different — something daring, unprecedented; something that simply does not belong to the world and its rational ideas, but comes from Heaven.

∞

Now, how does Jesus speak of *Providence?*

In the Sermon on the Mount, we read: "No man can serve two masters; for either he will hate the one and love the other, or else he will stand by the one and despise the other. You cannot serve God and mammon. Therefore I say to you, do not be anxious for your life, what you shall eat; nor yet for your body, what you shall put on. Is not life a greater thing than food, and the body than clothing? Look at the birds of the air; they do not sow, or reap, or gather into barns; yet your heavenly Father feeds them. Are not you of much more value than they? And which of you by being anxious about it can add to his stature a single cubit? And as for clothing, why are you anxious? Consider how the lilies of the field grow; they neither toil nor spin, yet I say to you that not even Solomon in all his glory was arrayed like one of these. But if God so clothes the grass of the field, which flourishes today but tomorrow is thrown into the oven, how much more you, O you of little faith! Therefore, do not be anxious, saying, 'What shall we eat?' or, 'What shall we drink?' or, 'What are we to put on?' (for after all these things the Gentiles seek); for your Father knows that you need all these things. But seek first the kingdom of God and His justice, and all these things shall be given to you besides. Therefore do not be anxious about tomorrow; for tomorrow will have anxieties of its own. Sufficient for the day is its own trouble."[40]

Does this sound like a mere "world order" — this challenge not to be anxious, not to ask, "What shall we eat, what shall we drink, and what shall we put on?" because the heathen trouble themselves about all these things? Was it not precisely those "heathen" who used to talk so eloquently of the "order" of the world? The Stoics, for instance, taught that the universe was a rational whole and that if one trusted the rational soul of this whole, all would be well. This must be something absolutely different.

But what? A fairy-tale existence, perhaps, in which food is wafted to the lazy and clothing grows on trees? Or a promise that the world shall lose the harshness of its realities and that it will be granted to the devout piously to put it right by their wishful thinking? By no means! On the contrary, everything that is said here about Providence must be understood in the light of that sentence near the end: "Seek first the kingdom of God and His justice, and all these things shall be given to you besides." "Thrown in with them," the actual words mean.

Everything hinges upon this. We are required to make the quest for the kingdom of God our first and most serious quest;

[40] Matt. 6:24-34.

to strive above all else to see that the kingdom of God comes and finds a place in our lives; to make it our first care that everything becomes as God wills it to be — the great God, whose thoughts are as high above those of man "as the Heaven is high above the earth."[41] As He plans and, as Creator, wills, so shall it be, despite the world and earthly reason. We must give ourselves bravely and completely to this end. We must transfer the center of our lives from self to God, and from this center think, judge, and act in accordance with the words of Christ. But this is difficult — extremely difficult.

It seems like folly, like cutting ourselves adrift from everything fixed and permanent. But if we achieve it, if we enter into an understanding with God to care for His kingdom, then God will care in a new, creative way for us. Life — which really, for all its vaunted rational order, cares nothing at all for man — rallies to us. Is this a miracle? Yes, from the merely worldly point of view, it is. In truth, it is a new creation, arising from the strength that can achieve such things — from the freely given love of God. The world is not ready formed. It lies plastic and pliant in His hand. If God's creative love is taken up by the loving solicitude and trust of the Christian, if man's free will is opened to it and gives it scope, then a new form of reality emerges from it. A new "order" originating from God comes into being, an order applied to the salvation of the new being. Life flows in his direction. He receives what he needs in the sight of God, even if it is by means of darkness and sorrow. In the measure that a person puts the quest for the kingdom of God first — "not in words but in deed and in

41 Ps. 102:11 (RSV = Ps. 103:11).

truth"[42] — he will be one with God in love. Then, by God's will, a new, all-embracing unity will arise. Events will coordinate themselves around such a person, and all that happens will be from God's love.

∞

Providence means something great and mysterious; it means that structure of existence which comes into being around the person who makes God's concern his own. The world around such a person becomes different. The "new Heaven and the new earth"[43] begin.

That, and not what the secularized thought of modern times has made of it, is what *Providence* means. And we will not debase the things of God. They shall keep their greatness and gloriousness in our eyes. If we feel ourselves too small for them, we will leave it at that; it is at least the truth. We will let the bountiful God be great in His richness, and acknowledge our littleness and our poverty in His sight. He will be merciful to us.

Providence does not mean the system of the world. That the universe has a system is something tremendous. The reflection that everything in it is coordinated and has its own law, and that we human beings are also so coordinated, must fill us with awe. But on such an order alone, our minds, hearts, and human dignity cannot thrive. A mere orderly system passes right through us — from the immeasurably distant into the immeasurably distant. To this order, we are only matter and tool.

[42] 1 John 3:18.
[43] Rev. 21:1.

It cares nothing for us, but only uses us. That is as it should be, and we do not ask for any fairy tales. But the order of Divine Providence means something different to us. It comes from the heart of God. It shines forth in the hearts of those of His creatures who have entered into the confederation of love with Him and collaborate with Him in care for His kingdom. It permeates these people — their opinions, their words, and their actions. It radiates from them into everything around them — people, things, and events. It takes hold of reality, orders it anew, and changes the world; not in fantasy, not as in a fairy tale, not by magic and witchcraft, but by the mighty operation of God's creative love and through the hearts of those who place themselves at His disposal.

It is from this angle that we must understand the petition for our daily bread. The person who speaks it is not concerned with the system of the universe. He is not reminding God that the rational order of existence should function properly today and tomorrow also with regard to his own food and clothing. He tries, rather, to fix his heart on "seeking the kingdom of God." He enters into a unity of understanding with God in this concern, in the place where he is and on the day through which he is living. And from there, he prays that the place where he is, the day that it is, the things that surround him now, may all obey the holy will of the Father, also in providing him with his bread and clothing and everything the heavenly Father knows that he needs.

"And forgive us our debts, as we also forgive our debtors"

The petitions of the second part of the Our Father stand there simple and transparent as the things of everyday life. But we have already reflected on the kind of life whose daily course they express — namely, the life of the child of God. That is indeed simple enough, something to be taken for granted — but by the grace of God. And if we examine this transparency thoughtfully, we very soon encounter the mysterious.

That has already been our experience with the first of these petitions. It will be in no way different with the following one: "And forgive us our debts, as we also forgive our debtors." Here we ask God to forgive us our debts. But have we already clearly grasped what asking the forgiveness of debt means? And what premise makes our petition meaningful?

∞

Debt means failure in regard to something obligatory; it means that something was done that was not permissible to do, or that something was not done that should have been done. But what authority decides what should and should not be done?[44]

In the ethical terminology of today, we speak of the "moral law." What this means becomes clear to us when we recall the various conceptions these words cover. Some think of the moral law as something in the nature of the laws of the state. These are legally instituted and binding for the citizen; by analogy, one thinks of a kind of moral law of the state, equally binding, but on another level of profundity, an invisible presence. Others, again, have a more abstract conception, somewhat on the lines of the rules of logic, which govern thought. As thought must follow these rules if it is not to err, so must action follow the moral law; otherwise it goes wrong.

There are still other and more clearly defined conceptions, but from those already outlined, it is clear that the petition for forgiveness simply does not make sense in relation to a "moral law." One cannot ask to be forgiven by the law of the state. Those who transgress it have to answer for their transgressions. One cannot ask to be forgiven by the laws of logic. Those who think wrongly can only try to extricate themselves as best they can from their error and take the consequences of what they have done wrongly. As long as we conceive of the binding authority only as an abstract law and of God only as its originator, a petition for forgiveness has no real sense. In

---

[44] The following illustrations overemphasize the premises in an effort to underline the religious note in the Christian doctrine of debt in contrast to the modern ethicism. This in no way implies raising an objection to the meaning of the ethical in the exact sense, or to the possibility of an authentic Christian ethic.

fact, we may even regard it as something questionable, if not cowardly and unethical. Before the mere "moral law," the conscience, with its responsibility, stands somehow alone and must answer for itself. To speak of forgiveness here is as if a person who had come of age were to put the responsibility for his moral failure on his father or mother. He has to cope with it himself.

For the believer, however, what binds in conscience is not only an abstract moral law but something living, which comes from God. It is the holy, the good, which impresses itself upon our inmost souls, and comes from God, and demands to be observed. God Himself is essential goodness, and He wills that we become good, as He is. Therefore, when we sin, we sin against this goodness. As soon as we conceive *debt* in this light and God as He appears in this order of ideas, does it not give a real meaning to the petition for forgiveness? Cannot the God so conceived forgive such a debt, if we leave to this word the authentic, original, and tangible meaning that it has in our minds and hearts? Would He not deny Himself in doing so? When He demands that good be done, He does not demand anything capricious, but rather what He Himself stands for. His own holiness is the good. He demands Himself, as it were, from man; and He must do this for His own sake. He cannot do otherwise, because He is God. But what, then, does *forgiveness* mean?

When we take the exalted character of this demand of God in all its seriousness, the idea of forgiveness is not yet fully explicit. It seems still to elude us. We have not yet gotten sufficiently far away from the abstract when we decide that the authority that binds us is not the "moral law" but the exacting holiness of God Himself. We must be still more concrete. Revelation tells us that the authority binding us is the living, holy will of God, which turns to all men and to me among them. This will of God has something completely personal about it. It does not only say that the commandment is valid, and it also binds you, as one of many; it says, in effect, that the commandment is meant for me in my particular life. In its deepest essence, it is not something that applies to all in an abstract way, and therefore also to me as an individual. True, it embraces the whole of humanity; but at the same time, it approaches me particularly in my one unique existence, and it does so, moreover, as the demand and concern of a heart to which I am dear.

Hence, what I owe retains its eternal and universal validity. Everything meant by the terms the "moral law," the "good," and the "demands of the All-Holy" — namely, the absolute, universally valid sovereignty — remains. Indeed, as soon as we probe more deeply, we recognize that only now is the real meaning of the moral law made evident: it posits a demand on our freedom that implies at the same time an obligation to a standard and a recognition of an order of values. There is by no means a self-evident law below, and above it a new and superfluous addition — the demand of love. Rather, the lower becomes evident only in light of the higher. Thus, the character of the law, with its sovereign necessity, obligating man's freedom without canceling it, only appears in its fullness when invested with the character of love. All its sternness remains, but its abstract character is gone, and it is drawn into the vital intimacy of person to person; or, better, of Creator to creature; or, better still, of the Father in Heaven to me, His son, His daughter.

Now we are down to bedrock: the "Thou shalt," the obligation laid upon me, arises from a relationship of love existing between God and me. His commandment is the way in which He loves me. It is the content of His love and at the same time the necessary premise that enables Him to love me.

∞

The petition for forgiveness hereby gains a deep, a very deep, meaning. When I obey God's demand, I have not only satisfied an impersonal law, but also fulfilled a relationship of love, which, of course, includes the perfection of every abstract law. And then its fruit is not only the consciousness of duty done and of a purer moral value, but also a greater nearness and a more living participation in God, who gives Himself to me. If, on the other hand, I do not obey, this involves not only wrongdoing in the abstract, but also sin against God's love, against my debt of love to God; and its fruit is alienation, estrangement, a drifting off into illusion, confusion and death.

Hence, we see that it is a case not of abstract "law" confronting "subject," but rather, of something vital and living — the most holy God, lovingly concerned for man; the address to God; the intimate association; the existence of man in and from God. A new dimension, if one may express it so, stands out in the relationship — the creative dimension.

Now, if I have failed, my failure is not in the abstract sphere between "law" and "subject," but in the living sphere of love between the "me" and the "Thee"; between the Word and the answer; in the holy interrelationship in which God comes to man and, in doing so, grants that man may go to Him. And there is a way — namely, penitence — in which I can become lovingly conscious of this debt, and with it enter into the vital relationship of love with God. Penitence is love related to debt. By penitence, I can ask God to forgive me my sins. In the end, His forgiving has the same meaning as His demand that we should do the right. In it, too, God's will to love is directed toward His creature, but now toward the creature that is guilty, "in debt."

But just as the compelling holiness of God was at the same time a living care for His creature, and the eternal validity of His commandment merged, as it were, into loving concern for the latter, so also does the divine condemnation of evil merge into loving concern for His child. If the person now enters into association with God's concern, a mystery of renewal takes place, wherein the "law" is satisfied and at the same time the salvation of the transgressor is engendered anew; and this is forgiveness.[45]

---

[45] These thoughts on love as the condition for forgiveness naturally are not meant as a contribution to the much-discussed questions regarding the different kinds of contrition and their relation to forgiveness. Here *love* is conceived in a broader sense, in contrast not to *fear*, but to the ethical attitude in the abstract. Christian fear itself comes within the domain of love as understood here — namely, that way of life that is formed in the individual by love of God and by the Christian belief in His love.

∞

But everything depends upon whether the sinner also is in a state of love; or, rather, it depends upon his returning to the bond of love from which he has divorced himself by his guilt.

Accordingly, the Our Father contains the admonition that the person asking for forgiveness should place himself in the state of love. But it does not trust him; therefore, it gives him an opportunity to test whether he is really in the state of love. It adds to this petition — and to no other — a condition: "Forgive us our debts, *as we also forgive our debtors.*" These two sentences, connected in this way, say: You may ask for forgiveness, but only if you are in a frame of mind that makes this request reasonable; not a state merely of moral shame, or depression, or fear of evil consequences, but of love. You will see clearly whether you have charity, if you ask yourself how you react to your fellow man when he has done you wrong.

∞

Here we recall something very significant. When the Lord was asked which was the first and greatest commandment of the Law, He replied, "Thou shalt love the Lord thy God with thy whole heart, and with thy whole soul, and with thy whole mind." "This," He added, "is the greatest and the first commandment." And then follows the striking sentence: "And the second is like it: Thou shalt love thy neighbor as thyself."[46] This is really strange. If the first-named commandment "is the first and the greatest," how then can a second one be "like it"?

[46] Matt. 22:37-39.

The Lord's Prayer

What does this mean? Obviously, that although at first sight the two commandments seem different, "to love God with thy whole mind" and "to love thy neighbor as thyself" are in truth one. Not merely the same, but one unit. I can love God only if I am prepared really to be what He created me to be. Now, He created me and wished me to be one of a community — a social being. He loves me in my individual self, but living among other people. Such is the love He requires of me — a mystery of union between Him and me, but for this very reason, also between me and others, and between Him and all. Love is a stream that flows from Him; it flows to me, but on through me to all others. It is the circulation of a blood that comes from the same heart, but flows through many members.

Hence, if I want to turn to Love with my sin — to that circulation that flows from the heart of God — and someone has sinned against me, someone in the same situation with me as I am with God, but I do not take him with me into the union of forgiveness, I erect a wall between him and me, but also between myself and God. No, actually, it is not like that. It is actually the same wall I allow to rise between my neighbor and myself that also rises up between myself and God; this shows that I am not in the state of love and cannot obtain forgiveness.

So the Our Father says that sin can be overcome only through union with God by love. Therefore, when you come to God with your sin, test yourself as to whether you are in that condition of love. You cannot know this as a man knows whether he is correctly dressed or not, or whether he has paid a debt; for love is a matter requiring faith. That God loves me, but also that I, by His grace, love Him — these are things not of this world; they are grace and mystery and therefore things that I can only devoutly hope. But if I sincerely forgive my neighbor his wrongdoing against me — insults, offenses, injuries, angry words, calumnies, harsh judgments, rude behavior, and everything by which he has done me wrong — this is my pledge that I may believe and hope that I love God.

I can have confidence that I am in God's love in the measure that my forgiveness of others is sincere. The more genuinely I overcome my inner resistance; the more sincerely I try to overcome my hatred or aversion; the more deeply I allow real, genuine, liberating forgiveness to reach down to the depths of the wrong he has done me, the more confidently I may hope to be in God's love and, consequently, to have my plea for forgiveness heard. "Thou shalt love the Lord thy God, and thy neighbor as thyself." Here, this means: You shall forgive others as you wish God to forgive you. You shall do to others what you ask may be done to you, so that the blood of love, through which alone forgiveness comes, may travel full circle.

∞

But, of course, we have forgotten one thing. The first premise that this petition requires before we can even dare to utter it is that we admit sincerely before God that we are guilty. And that cannot be taken for granted.

For the person who has obviously and palpably sinned, this means that he must really admit his guilt; he must cast aside the self-assertiveness that would make him seek to justify himself, the cowardice that would make him shirk responsibility for his act, the secret cunning that would try to get around the worst point. For the person who leads a "good life," this admission means realizing how paltry his "goodness" is, how much egotism and narrowness, insincerity and mixed motives are mingled with it. He must realize how often his "being good" was due only to favorable circumstances that shielded him; chance, which carried him on; privilege, which spared him. But deeper still, he must realize and acknowledge that he and his good life are bound up in the unity of guilt of mankind everywhere; that all his good and evil works signify, in the last resort, only a difference within the great circle of sinful humanity in which all of us who "are wanting in justice before God"[47] stand, in need of forgiveness.

Note how the petition of the Our Father warns us: to acknowledge our guilt for the sins that we have definitely committed; to recognize the magnitude of the wrongdoing we often regard as trifling; to see the sins that lie under our virtues and righteousness. But, over and above all this, it warns us to realize not only that we have committed sins, but also that we are sinners and, with all that we are, stand guilty in the sight of God. It warns us not to withdraw ourselves from the mass of humanity in an aristocracy of self-righteousness, but honestly to take our place in the universal responsibility of humanity. It warns us to pray not only about our own individual guilt but also about the guilt that encompasses all: that God may open our eyes to it, may break its spell, help us to rise from that guilt and come back to Him again and again.

[47]Cf. Ezra 9:15.

Being a Christian means just that: continually rising up out of guilt — the one great common guilt, together with all it includes of our individual guilt — to come to God and beg Him for forgiveness; and it means being gradually transformed by this continually renewed forgiveness.

The Sixth Petition

"And lead us not into temptation"

Our meditations on the Our Father are drawing to a close. Two petitions remain to be considered. They are joined in a single sentence; the first of them is "And lead us not into temptation."

In the course of these meditations, we have found again and again that, from an apparently intimate knowledge, due no doubt to frequent repetition of the prayer, we were quickly led into unsuspected depths and mysteries. Now, we still remember that petition with which we sought a way into the Our Father. It showed us that we have before us, not a system of doctrine, but rather a living fabric, as it were. One thought led on to another, defined it, determined it, and carried it forward. One layer of reality pointed to another at greater depth; this one led to one still more submerged, and so on. The interplay of various movements became manifest; the will decided, the heart stirred, and a creative process formed the inner man. A whole existence — the authentic, Christian existence in which redeemed man stands in relation to his fellow being, to created things, and all together stand before God — found expression. We had expected that the Our Father would show us what it means to live as a Christian; that it would bring home to us what it means to be a Christian in today's world, what realities shape the Christian character, and in what convictions the Christian lives. And, in fact, each petition, from a particular point of view, has led us down to the very roots of that existence.

The sentence with which we are dealing now, "Lead us not into temptation," will do the same. Once more, we shall strip off layer after layer of the living whole to reach the core. In doing so, we shall come upon thoughts that may startle us at first; but to live the Christian life is not a harmless matter. And no purpose is served in glossing over what is dark and difficult, for that only makes it erupt all the more surely, but in secret and poisonous form. However, as soon as we face these difficult things squarely with the strength of Christian faith, the glory of the love of God will appear in all its radiance.

The petition says: "Lead us not into temptation." What can this signify? It might be interpreted to mean that God should not bring us into the possibility of sinning. But it cannot mean that, for we are already situated in that possibility, and to extricate us from it would require a miracle. Once God has created things, strong in being and rich in meaning, the possibility exists once and for all that man may take them as existing in their own right, self-created and self-sufficing. And since man has been created, and established in the independence of his intellectual life to confront the world on his own — to discern, judge, and decide for himself — the possibility also exists, once and for all, that he may make himself the center of his universe, take himself and all created things in the universe as the essential element of being, sufficient to itself. That would be sin; but the act of the first man was sin, and sin is committed over and over again in the wrongdoing of all of us.

Seen in this light, the petition can mean only that God may grant that this happening, which is potential by necessity, may not become act.

∞

This, certainly, is part of the petition, but there is much more to it, and we must probe more deeply. The petition could also envisage the situation in which the possibilities of sinning, inherent in existence, might crowd upon the person and become imperative. In such a case, things would so encompass the person, events would so direct themselves toward him, happenings would so confront him, that the choice between good and evil would clamor for decision; and not just in the simple form of either-or, but in such a way that evil would come dangerously near. The forces of passion, sloth, and rebellion inherent in man would awaken and press the individual into action. That would be temptation in the true sense.

Temptation can harass frightfully. The Books of Kings tell of Saul, that passionate and unruly man; how he assembles his army against the Philistines and is waiting impatiently for the moment when he may strike. This he must not do before solemn sacrifice has been offered. But Samuel the prophet has given orders to wait until he himself arrives to offer it. And he has not come. The enemy are pressing more and more fiercely, and Saul's men are losing courage and beginning to flee. But still Samuel does not come. Time is running short. Finally Saul gives orders to prepare the sacrifice. He is still speaking when the prophet appears on the scene and brings him the tidings that he has failed to stand the test and is rejected by God.[48]

It can happen to anyone, and it can happen again and again, that the multifarious distractions and allurements of life, which no foresight can guard us against, may turn the possibility of sin into urgent danger and, from that, into fierce temptation. And so the prayer pleads: Deliver us from it! Thou hast the right to put us to the test. Thou hast the right to lead us into the perils of decision. But, Lord, consider our weakness!

And so the petition would be a humble recognition of the truth and an appeal to God's mercy.

But there is still another layer of meaning. Can God permit temptation to become so severe that we *must* fall? If we deny that He can, and that, in view of His divinity, He may, we are making God innocuous.

It is certain that no hour ever stands isolated. It is always woven into the whole fabric of life. Today's temptation grows from our doings of yesterday and before that, back and back through all the years past. What I have done or neglected to do throughout time is still there. It has become incorporated into my living being as weakness or strength, protection or threat. It has penetrated into the realities surrounding me, the things and the people, the circumstances and the associations. And the present hour, with its temptations, is the distillation of all that has happened. Thus it may well be that the failure, levity, disobedience, sloth, and passion of many past hours find

[48] 1 Kings 13:5-14 (RSV = 1 Sam. 13:5-14).

their retribution and punishment in a temptation that it is beyond my strength to resist.

It would be dangerous to think that this could not happen. This petition of the Lord's Prayer knows that it can happen and that God is only being just when He permits it. But it calls upon that quality in God that is greater than His justice — namely, His mercy.

Therefore it is a plea for God's patience. How great a thought that is — the patience of God! Only the Almighty can be completely imperturbable. Only the Eternal One can wait without hurry. Only He, the Lord, the Sovereign One, to whom all things belong and whom all things obey, can wait for His creature at all the turnings of wrong roads, and stand at the end of all labyrinthine ways. He can hear the plea for forgiveness again and again. It does not upset Him. It does not disturb the decrees of His justice. It does not make Him impatient. It is only the cause, ordained by Himself, of completing, in calm and holy freedom, the works of forgiveness and love that, with the triumphant glory of the Creator, go beyond everything that can be explained from the human viewpoint as possible or impossible, right or wrong — into the "newness of life,"[49] the life of grace and of the Holy Spirit. The "God and Father of Jesus Christ,"[50] to whom the Lord's Prayer turns, can call from the abyss the person who, from the human point of view, is at the end of his tether, and tell him that he shall begin anew. When the weakness and wrongdoing of the past should have been distilled, according to the ordinary laws of justice,

[49] Rom. 6:4.
[50] Cf. Col. 1:3; 1 Pet. 1:3.

into a mortal temptation, God can so renew the heart that it gains strength to overcome the temptation.

God of patience! Let us not fall from Thy calm and unerring hands!

∞

Have we now reached the heart of the matter, or does it go down still deeper to the roots of our existence? How about the ninth chapter of the letter to the Romans, which speaks of the dark mystery of predestination? That God knows everything; that nothing happens that is not His will; that nothing has its reason except in God, because everything that is, is only from God and so also our eternal destiny? And that man has no possibility of appealing to any tribunal of justice above God? "Does the object molded say to him who molded it, 'Why hast thou made me thus?' Or is not the potter master of his clay, to make from the same mass one vessel for honorable, another for ignoble use? But what if God, wishing to show His wrath and to make known His power, endured with much patience vessels of wrath, made for destruction, that He might show the riches of His glory upon vessels of mercy, which He has prepared unto glory?"[51]

All efforts to penetrate the mystery, with fine distinctions, are in vain in the end. Indeed, there is a danger of making God seem small, hanging man in midair, so to speak, as something semi-independent, midway between creature and noncreature.

No, an inscrutable mystery reigns here, and let us let it be! Having established with certainty that "God wills not the

[51] Rom. 9:20-23.

death of the sinner, but that he be converted and live";[52] that all evil comes only from man, not from the most holy God; that the eternal damnation of man is therefore his own fault and that God is only just when He pronounces that verdict; after we have exerted our understanding to the utmost and drawn all possible distinctions, the fact remains that all that happens is finally not only from God, but embedded in the mystery of His decrees.

This is a dark mystery. It has weighed heavily on many a mind and darkened many a soul. A gloomy theology has arisen out of it. But we cannot do away with all this by denying what is. Rather, we must understand it in all its Christian depths and with all its related doctrine. Divine predestination and predetermination become something frightful against which our God-given human dignity and our longing for salvation alike revolt as soon as the question is falsely posed. We must therefore ask: Who is the God from whose decrees everything comes? Answer: He who is love itself; He who Christ says is our Father. The decree remains, and the inscrutable mystery remains. But He who decrees is the Loving One, and the inscrutability of His decrees is the mystery of His love.

This is what makes everything different — everything; not different as if something were struck out, but on the contrary, by everything being accepted, embraced, and permeated in a manner that transmutes it. It is into this that the petition of the Our Father leads.

But we must cooperate with this mystery, not only state it. Mere stating does not help. Thinking only points the way.

[52] Cf. Ezek. 18:23.

Everything becomes real only when it is actualized in the mind.

∞

Then we find true blessedness. Our Christian life is grace; but this means that it is not ours by right or by achievement, but by God's free gift. It comes from His love.

Therein consists the blessedness of Christianity; the mysterious and daring element that makes it beautiful beyond the realms of thought. For grace, *charisma*, does indeed signify something that is outside the sphere of effort and obligation, the free gift of God; this is its attraction and beauty, that it is given wholly gratuitously by God's benevolence. Precisely herein lies the blessedness of the Christian state — that it comes from love. Therefore the Christian is watchful with holy concern that everything does indeed come from God's love. But this is possible only if it comes purely from His free gift and is nowhere hedged in by rights or securities; in other words, if it really remains grace. Indeed, so anxious is the Christian that this should be so, that he gives up everything that means "security." For security signifies right, guarantee, constraint. So he throws the last scrap of it away. Thus does the Christian heart admit that God makes man, decides what he is to be, and directs his destiny as He will; and he renounces all opposition and all right of appeal. Herein lies the true meaning of the idea of predestination: it is the final guarantee that all comes from God's freedom, that all remains a matter of grace — because only so can it be love.

The thought of predestination is a thought of love. As soon as one conceives it otherwise, it becomes something frightful.

With it, the Christian says to God: Thou art the Lord. Thou art free, also in regard to me. With my being and my destiny I come from Thy decree. Thy decree is supreme. Whatever its verdict may be, it is right. There is no right above it against which it must be measured; on the contrary, all right begins with it. Therefore I desire that it be accomplished, just as it will, of itself, in pure freedom. I long for heavenly bliss, and Thou art it. But I can possess Thee only if Thou Thyself givest Thyself; and that is love. But how is one to love, except in freedom? Therefore I take the venture of Thy freedom, that Thy love may come to me from it; Thy freedom, which Thou hast told me is called "grace." I desire the bliss of Heaven only out of love, and so I venture the freedom of love, with all its consequences, which include the possibility of failure.

Such thinking is audacious. One cannot reduce it to a system. It is not a doctrinal structure of *ifs* and *therefores* but a dialogue between the child of God and his Father — a prayer of love. Whenever anyone has tried to reduce it to a system, the result has been wretched, and the Church has had to condemn it. One cannot know these truths in the abstract; one must realize them in prayer and in love. That is why the Christian lets go of everything that spells security, rights, and demonstrable common sense. But it is precisely in doing this that he achieves harmony with the love of God, that he achieves a union that is stronger than all security. It is as if he let go of the earth and, in loosening his hold, is able to rise freely. In the measure that he renounces security and surrenders himself freely to the love of God, he experiences a confidence beyond all reason and a hope beyond all security. And then a new kind of reason, which has been released into the space opened up by love, comes into his experience.

That is the way it is, and the way it should be.

Thou, O God, art indeed love. Thou hast indeed created me. There will be no more demands on my part, no more refusals; no more reckoning; no more thoughts of rights. All that is done with! Thou alone sufficeth, O God!

The petition leads to profound depths — to the inmost depths of the strength from which the Christian draws his God-directed life. Once you accept this thought, you will understand why the ninth through eleventh chapters of Paul's letter to the Romans, so dark and terrifying in certain parts, culminate in the outburst: "Oh, the depth of the riches of the wisdom and of the knowledge of God! How incomprehensible are His judgments and how unsearchable His ways! For who has known the mind of the Lord, or who has been His counselor? Or who has first given to Him, that recompense should be made him? For from Him, and through Him and unto Him are all things. To Him be the glory forever. Amen."[53]

---

[53]Rom. 11:33-36.

The Seventh Petition

"But deliver us from evil"

And now we come to the seventh and last petition. It is linked to the petition last spoken of, "Lead us not into temptation," which is followed by the words "But deliver us from evil."

What is this evil from which we should ask to be delivered, as the Our Father teaches us?

What evil is it? The only difficulty in answering this question seems to be that there are so many evils to choose from. We do not have to make special efforts to find them; they press on us from all sides: sickness and want, sorrow, misfortune, and death. Our own experience and the knowledge of our heart incite us to turn with all our afflictions to the Lord of the world and to beg Him to help us.

But we have already seen, in the prayer for our daily bread, that we must not take this supplication at face value. It is not as if we knew that there are doctors to cure sickness, and that we go to God because He is the best doctor; or as if there were authorities to deal with economic difficulties, and we go to Him as to the supreme and most reliable authority. We have already seen that Christian supplication goes beyond the mere asking for help from a benevolently disposed supreme power that would deal with the things of the world as in a fairy tale, making them easy and unreal. Nor does it voice the illusion of naïve, simple-minded people, which would vanish once the eye had seen clearly.

We have seen that Christian petition addresses itself to Divine Providence. But what Providence is, is made clear by these words: "Seek first the kingdom of God and His justice, and all these things shall be given to you besides."[54] To be sure, Providence is being accomplished by God in man all the time, but it becomes what it really signifies only in the measure that man enters into agreement with God in concern for His kingdom. Then the world around him changes. To him who really loves God, "all things work together for good,"[55] and "all these things shall be added unto him."

So it is here, too. All petitions that God may preserve us from evil come within the framework of Providence and have as a premise the premise of Providence itself: concern for the kingdom of God.

∞

But there is more than that in the words about evil. It is not for nothing that the petition for deliverance from it is linked with the prayer that asks God for forgiveness for sin. One

---

[54] Matt. 6:33.
[55] Rom. 8:28.

needs only to examine the connection briefly to see that both sentences refer basically to the same thing: evil is what comes from sin.

Let us consider our daily experience:

When I am incensed against my neighbor and feel hatred or repugnance for him, the image of him does not strike me with its original sharpness. It has to go through a filter, as it were — a bad filter in which the good is drained off or diluted but the evil is concentrated. His words do not reach me in their true tone; they are transposed to another pitch. I do not trust his friendliness; I read into it bad intentions, mental reservations, ulterior motives that are not there at all. Everything that comes from him I construe as unfriendly or inimical, so that often it seems as if some evil spell poisoned and distorted everything. And if my neighbor is not firmly anchored in righteousness and in genuine goodwill, my attitude toward him will eventually cause him to adopt the same attitude toward me.

Like evokes like. Unfriendliness is answered by unfriendliness; aversion by aversion; wickedness by wickedness. So there is plenty of evil about! And from where has it come if not from the wickedness in me — and from the wickedness in my neighbor, which has been aroused by mine?

When the heart is weary, even the most beautiful things are covered with a veil. Words that should stir and hearten remain lifeless. Events that should thrill leave one cold. Everything tender and gay, which should rise up freely and beautifully, falls spent to the ground. The joyful and generous is discouraged. The exalted becomes trivial. All this, too, is a great evil, but it comes from the heart and its wickedness.

The Lord's Prayer

When a person is in the grip of passion, it rages in him and makes him restless. His daily life exasperates him. Passion devalues people and things in his eyes; it makes his duties dull and obnoxious. It destroys the order in his thoughts and feelings, and drives him to rebellion; it confuses everything. It hurts, oppresses, allures. Evil encompasses him on all sides, but it comes from the evil in his mind.

∾

How much more of this sort could be said!

The world does not exist and subsist by itself; it is no ready-made house into which one can enter, no perfect order of things with which one can fall in. To be sure, it may be that, too; but this is not what we have in mind when we consider the term *world* more seriously.

This world exists for and by man. It has two centers: one that lies in things, the other that lies in man. Or, more precisely, it lies in the particular person in question; in his eyes, which see things; in his will, which encounters them; in his heart, which feels them. Only in the reciprocal relationships of him to things, and of things to him, does it become "world." And this is not the case in such a way that it is experienced only "subjectively," in the disparaging sense of the word, as something to be set aside. On the contrary, the world, the world of men, comes into being only as man and things encounter each other; man forms the world in conformity with his own specific being. Consequently, if there is evil in him, there will be evil in the world.

No pious speculations are implied here; we are concerned with the actual truth about the world of men. It is certainly wrong to say that "outside" of man there is only a confusion of sense appeals that have to be reduced to order by the thinking and seeing human mind. No, outside of man are real things, and between them and the person, there is contact. But the true significance of the term *world* is still not the sum of those things that are mirrored, assessed, and comprehended by the individual; rather, it lies in the vital interplay of thing and person that arises in this encounter. The resulting effect is determined by what man permits, decides, or influences. The world that God intended in His creation comes into being only in conjunction with man. God has called man to perfect the world in this encounter. Hence, the outcome of this encounter is determined by what man himself is: the good in him becomes the good and the luminous in the world; the evil in him becomes the evil of the world.

The petition of which we are speaking therefore means: Deliver us from the evil in ourselves, so that it may not become the evil of the world. Teach us to understand that evil comes from the evil in man, from the evil in me. Teach me to understand that the world can continually renew itself, the good outside of man coming from the good within him — from the heart that is redeemed and that has received from Thee by faith and Baptism the seed of the new creation. Thus shall arise the "new Heaven and the new earth," which no evil oppresses any longer, because there is no longer any evil residing in them, but only good aroused by the good; blessedness outside from holiness within, "for the first Heaven and the first earth" have indeed "passed away."[56]

[56]Rev. 21:1.

The Lord's Prayer

We spoke of the evil that comes from the evil in the individual personality. That was a first intimation that leads on to further associations.

A spoken word does not fade into nothingness when its sound fades away. It enters into the consciousness of those who hear it; leaves its stamp on the inmost being of its speaker; continues to operate in the memory and the heart, in the effects it has produced. It becomes a part of reality. It is the same with everything we do. As soon as it is launched from its origin in our freedom, it becomes a part of reality, continuing to run its course and to take effect, on the rails of existence. From this is woven, in the world, what we call "history."

An evil that is oppressing me now does not come out of the blue. It comes from words that were spoken before; from ineptitude, negligence, and evil deeds of the past. The wickedness of the heart takes tangible shape in the world. It becomes distilled into evil, and emerges to confront someone somewhere else in the form of scandal, hindrance, or an oppressive atmosphere. The evil I have to contend with is a distillation from past evil that comes from others or myself. This evil, then, enkindles further evil, which bears new seed of evil; one arises continually out of the other, and so the evil chain is unending.

As with our personal history, so it is with history in the large sense. Wars are not started by the force of nature, but by selfishness everywhere: by hardness that thought only of its own advantage; by indifference to the fate of others; by greed for power; by vainglory; by inordinate ambition; by greed for possessions; by the mysterious urge to oppress others, to torture, to destroy. When the last war started, its force had been accumulated from the wickedness of millions of hearts, from the evil in the depths of the human race. The suffering that oppresses mankind everywhere confronts the individual as a universal evil; it does not originate from the earth or from the necessities of nature, but from humanity. When we ask ourselves whether the earth has room and bread for all, there can be only one answer. Nevertheless, many have neither room nor bread, because the real evil does not stem from nature, but from the coldness and hardness of selfishness, the negligence of the indolent, the thoughtlessness of the superficial and pleasure-loving. Therefore, the petition "Deliver us from evil" means: Grant that the frightful chain reaction may be broken by which evil continually arises out of wickedness and, in turn, engenders new evil. But it can be broken only in each heart that gives itself to God and undertakes to care that His will be done.

True, a tangled skein of evil exists, but to be entangled in it is not blind fate. Redemption has come to all and can be realized in each one. The freedom of the children of God can be awakened in man from God, and the power of the Redemption, emanating from liberated hearts, can penetrate the chain of universal evil.

Paul tells us that all evil comes from sin. This is the one great sin of all: the sin that happened when the first man — and in him, all mankind — broke away from loving union with the will of God, and so humanity fell into abandonment, desolation, ruin, and death. This sin lives in every heart. It continues to operate in the personal sins of us all, and engenders new sin. For there are not so many separate and independent sins; rather, the sin of the individual is embedded, as it were, in sin itself; in that frightful, mysterious unity, that bondage and power of which the letter to the Romans speaks. On each individual, the sin of all weighs, and all are somehow or other affected by the sin each commits. Hence, the plea for deliverance from evil becomes a petition on behalf of all humanity. In it, the individual brings before God the guilt of humanity from which the evils of man's life come; each individual brings the guilt and the misery of all, his own included. It is a petition for deliverance from evil as a whole.

But with this thought, we have reached out beyond the more intimate and daily aspect into the Christian life as a whole, and here the thought reaches its culmination.

The deliverance from evil meant in the petition does not refer, in the last analysis, to secular time at all. It is that delivery or redemption that will come when Christ appears. The consciousness of this pervades the whole petition. Sin and evil are of such unimaginable magnitude, what is called sin has so pervaded the work of God to its very roots, that genuine salvation can come only when God brings the world back to the unity of His holy will through death, resurrection, and the Last Judgment, after sin and evil have run their course. The last word in all Christian thought, the final goal of all Christian solicitude, no longer applies to the temporal universe and historical time. In the end, the Christian life is focused not on what will happen when, scientifically speaking, the earth will be engulfed by the new ice age, or however else the "end of the world" can be imagined in the astrophysical view. It is focused on the Lord's Second Coming, on the third intervention of God. (The second intervention was the Redemption, and the first, the creation.)

∞

At the end of Revelation, the cry "Come, Lord Jesus!"[57] arises out of the company of those awaiting the Lord. Out of the depths of the petition "Deliver us from evil," the selfsame cry resounds. Ceaselessly, from countless hearts, there rises up to God a petition of which many do not know the inmost meaning. But the depth is there all the same, heaving up its darkness. It is the inmost core of the created world, which sighs for God, and "groans and travails in pain"[58] for the coming of the last things. It is this depth that calls to God in the petition.

It is the deepest layer of Christian consciousness that calls out here — the layer that knows that the world cannot be patched up, that it cannot by positive thinking be turned to the good. Too much of unthinkable magnitude has happened. What God has staked against it is the full measure of His love. The immeasurable catastrophe of sin, the frightful chain of wickedness and evil that runs through history: after man, individually and generically, has done his utmost to defeat it, the realization breaks through that only God can truly do something about it. And the longing swells for the coming of that which not only can turn all things to the good, but also leads into the new: the end of time, which is the breakthrough of the eternal.

[57]Rev. 22:20.
[58]Rom. 8:22.

Amen

Our meditations on the Lord's Prayer have reached their end.

First, we sought a gateway that would lead into the fruitful profundity of the Our Father, and we found it in the petition that the will of God be done, that basic Christian petition in which the supplicant, taught by God, joins in the concern for the will of the Father, and thereby enters into an understanding with God Himself. And so we arrived at the heart of the Lord's Prayer — the union of the Christian with his Father in Heaven.

Then, each separate sentence opened up the meaning of the whole. The petitions of the first part initiated us into the mystery of the name of God; into the mystery of His kingdom; into the mystery of His will and of the significance of this will in Heaven and on earth. Then we came to the second part of the prayer, which speaks with such simplicity and clarity of everyday life. But we realized that it must be interpreted in the light of the first part of the prayer and that accordingly, the simple clarity of existence that appears in it is something very great indeed — namely, the simplicity of the child of God who draws life from the mysteries implicit in the first petitions. And as we considered the various petitions one by one, each time, it did not take long to experience the power of their holy depth.

Christian usage concludes the hallowed sentences of the Lord's Prayer with one last word: *Amen*. Let us also consider the meaning of this.

∞

We meet the word on the lips of the Lord. He pronounces it at particularly solemn moments: "Amen, amen — truly, truly — I say unto you."[59] It originates from the prayer language of the Old Testament and signifies a protestation, a confirmation that what is said is true, true before God, strictly and devoutly affirmed. It is in this sense that it stands also at the end of the Lord's Prayer. In what, now, does this affirmation and confirmation consist?

∞

When Martha, "anxious and troubled about many things," busies herself as housewife, making everything ready for the Lord, Jesus says to her, "Only one thing is needful!" But meanwhile, Mary, intent only upon Him, and sitting quietly at His feet, has "chosen the best part."[60] This we are told, and it will always be the better part to remain turned to God with one's whole being. But Christ has also said something else:

[59] John 1:51.
[60] Luke 10:41-42.

"Not everyone who says to me, 'Lord, Lord,' shall enter the kingdom of Heaven; but he who does the will of my Father in Heaven shall enter the kingdom of Heaven."[61] This points out to us the danger of sterility threatening a life devoted exclusively to prayer: the danger of contemplating and not acting; of indulging the feelings instead of exerting the will; of passive contentment, irresolution, lack of deeds. The Amen reminds us that the right prayer is also an action, although not an exterior but an interior one — an interior consummation. Praying is not standing aside from reality, dreaming and longing; on the contrary, it demands the whole person: his contemplation, the tension of his will, and the movement of his heart. A genuine movement must take place, in which the heart opens and tends toward God; there must be stoutness of character, translating insight into responsibility; there must be resolution that ensures that all this is not a passing attitude, soon to be dissipated, but a solid frame of mind that finds expression in everyday action.

All this is implied in the Amen at the end. It seals the seriousness of the prayer.

The Lord has said, "The kingdom of Heaven has been enduring violent assault, and the violent have been seizing it by force."[62] The kingdom of Heaven is not something that falls out of the blue, as things in fairy tales do. Nor is it something that by necessity evolves from the nature of man. It comes from God and is in a continual state of coming, but man must seize hold of it and draw it to himself. He must take the risk of

[61] Matt. 7:21.
[62] Matt. 11:12.

commitment. But there is much in his nature that resists it: desires he must renounce if he really wants the kingdom of God; passions that must be kept in check or resolved if the kingdom of God is to have scope within him. We are bound on all sides; our fetters hold us fast and resist being severed. Selfishness holds us tight and will not let us go.

This is where the "violence" that must be used to reach the kingdom of God comes in. We must break through ourselves; we must break the fetters that bind us and the trammels that encompass us: human respect, attachments, settled circumstances, relationships, habits, and alleged duties.

The Amen signifies this determination. It calls it forth and seals it. The whole of the Our Father revolves around the kingdom of God; it expresses the consciousness of its nearness and the hope of its coming. And the Amen says, "I want it to come." It reaches out toward it: "Be it so!" And it throws its force back into the petitions that have preceded it; they shall have been prayed in the fervor and holy resolve of that Amen.

∞

The first proclamation of our Lord was "The kingdom of God is at hand. Repent and believe in the gospel."[63]

The kingdom of God does not fall into our lap like a gift in a dream. It does not take possession of us like a spell. The gospel calls to us, announced by the words, spoken and written, of those who teach it; by events; by experience; and by personal contacts that move the heart. The joyful tidings of the gospel call to us, and we must believe them. But to be able

[63] Mark 1:15.

to believe them, we must at least be ready to repent, or else we remain deaf, obtuse, fettered, and closed to them. We, who are always turning away from God, must turn back and go to Him. Our hearts, distracted and given to things and people, must be surrendered to Him. We must bow our will, so full of rebellion, beneath His will.

All this is easy to say, but inexpressibly difficult to do. And it is difficult not only because there is so much in us that resists — the will shuts itself up, the passions sit tight, and our inner nature is fastened into our old ways with a thousand roots — but also because our whole nature is in a continual state of flux. We notice how much this is so only when we occasionally try to probe it in depth. Is it an easy matter to say the *yes* of consent to an obligation so that it is truly binding? To put our whole being into the consent? To do so without any mental reservations and without leaving open some side issue? To do so in order that loyalty is preserved whole, with no seepage of any kind? Is it easy to reach a true conviction? Not just an insight or intimation or realization of what is right, but a genuine conviction, which engages the force of our character, our honor, the truth of our fate — for do not finding the truth and living by it decide our spiritual destiny? It is anything but easy; it is extremely difficult for us to grasp the truth with our whole being and faithfully incorporate it into our lives.

But when it is a question of God and His kingdom, of Him who is manifest and yet so hidden; who gives salvation and satisfies the heart; and from whom nevertheless our inmost being continually shrinks, to reach instead toward all the color and richness of the world around us — is it an easy matter to achieve a clear and firm state of commitment and loyalty to this? For God and His kingdom are eternal and infinite, while we feel ourselves transitory and small. How can we grasp that measureless immensity? Our limitations and His infinity: how can they ever converge? Are our capacities not always over-taxed? And in spite of our goodwill, is there not always an unbridgeable gap of incomprehension? Is there not some doubt that has no basis other than the limited strength of mind and heart, which cannot bear the might of the truth in question? Is there not an insecurity in our firmest grasp; a hesitation; an inability to make the total surrender; a clumsiness; a weight; a restriction in spite of our willingness?

As we consider this, the significance of the Amen becomes quite clear to us; it draws a line to our endless questioning and wavering; sets a boundary to our ceaseless state of flux; decides between yes and no, and holds to our decision.

∞

The Amen says, "Be it so."

The Amen changes the instability of the creature into fidelity to God.

The Amen brings the creature's flight from God to a stand-still. This must be sincerely and bravely done, "with the whole heart, and with the whole mind, and with all one's strength."[64] It must be continually renewed. After each fall, it must be raised up again; it must be confirmed in steadfastness after lapses into indifference and thoughtlessness; it must be taken up again and affirmed after being forgotten. Again and again,

[64]Cf. Matt. 22:37; Mark 12:30.

we must overcome doubt, strengthen the wavering mind, and conquer weariness.

But there is one doubt we have to let pass, for it comes from faith itself. Every Amen remains valueless unless God Himself pronounces it. We say "forever," and already life is at work, nibbling at this "forever," and after a time, it has gone to pieces. We say, "I stand by it absolutely," and do not realize that already currents within us are flowing in other directions, eroding our words, until one fine day we find our position changed, not knowing how we got there. We are touched to the core, shaken, overwhelmed, and think the Absolute itself has taken possession of our spirit. But life goes on with the force of events, griefs, and vexations; the sigh of the wind and the song of a bird blot out what was once so powerful. One day, it is all gone, and we can no longer understand how we could once have thought that we had any share in what endures.

No, indeed! If it is to be really Amen, God Himself must speak it. He who is fidelity itself must ground us in fidelity. He who is truth itself must enlighten our minds. He must take hold of us and give us that strength that endures in all the ups and downs of life and rises again and again when everything threatens to sink.

The Amen is our way of saying that the supplicant is breaking through mental sloth and sterility to vital spiritual action. It expresses his determination to see the kingdom of God realized; his will to put an end to his fickleness and change it into resolution and constancy. Having done all this, the Amen itself turns into a petition: "Lord, do Thou say, 'Amen!' Bring the Amen to life within me: as truth, deeply rooted; fidelity that does not waver; resolution that does not tire!"

Romano Guardini
(1885-1968)

Although he was born in Verona, Italy, Msgr. Romano Guardini grew up in Mainz, Germany, where his father was serving as Italian consul. Since his education and formation were German, he decided to remain in Germany as an adult.

After studying chemistry and economics as a youth, Guardini turned to theology and was ordained to the priesthood in 1910. From 1923 to 1939 (when he was expelled by the Nazis), Msgr. Guardini occupied a chair created for him at the University of Berlin as "professor for the philosophy of religion and Catholic *Weltanschauung*." After the war, similar positions were created for him, first at the University of Tübingen and then at the University of Munich (1948-1963). Msgr. Guardini's extremely popular courses in these universities won him a reputation as one of Germany's most remarkable and successful Catholic educators. As a teacher, writer, and speaker, he was notable for being able to detect and nurture those elements of spirituality that nourish all that is best in the life of Catholics.

The Lord's Prayer

After the war, Msgr. Guardini's influence grew to be enormous, not only through his university positions, but also through the inspiration and guidance he gave to the postwar German Catholic youth movement, which enlivened the faith of countless young people.

Msgr. Guardini's writings include works on meditation, education, literature, philosophy, theology, and art. Among his many books, perhaps the most famous is *The Lord*, which has been continuously in print in many languages since its first publication in 1937. Even today, countless readers continue to be transformed by these beautiful books, which combine a profound thirst for God with depth of thought and a delightful perfection of expression.

The works of Msgr. Guardini are indispensable reading for all Christians who want to remain true to the Faith and to grow holy in our age of skepticism and corrosive doubt.

Sophia Institute Press

Sophia Institute is a nonprofit institution that seeks to restore man's knowledge of eternal truth, including man's knowledge of his own nature, his relation to other persons, and his relation to God.

Sophia Institute Press serves this end in numerous ways. It publishes translations of foreign works to make them accessible for the first time to English-speaking readers. It brings back into print books that have been long out of print. And it publishes important new books that fulfill the ideals of Sophia Institute. These books afford readers a rich source of the enduring wisdom of mankind.

Sophia Institute Press makes high-quality books available to the general public by using advanced technology and by soliciting donations to subsidize our general publishing costs.

Your generosity can help us provide the public with editions of works containing the enduring wisdom of the ages. Please send your tax-deductible contribution to the address on the following page.

The members of the Editorial Board of Sophia Institute Press welcome questions, comments, and suggestions from all our readers.

For your free catalog, call:

Toll-free: 1-800-888-9344

or write:

Sophia Institute Press

Box 5284

Manchester, NH 03108

Sophia Institute is a tax-exempt institution as defined by the Internal Revenue Code, Section 501(c)(3). Tax I.D. 22-2548708.

— Notes and Meditations —

— Notes and Meditations —

— Notes and Meditations —

— Notes and Meditations —

— Notes and Meditations —

— Notes and Meditations —

— Notes and Meditations —

— Notes and Meditations —

— Notes and Meditations —

— Notes and Meditations —